Acoustic Design
for the
HOME STUDIO

by
Mitch Gallagher

COURSE TECHNOLOGY
CENGAGE Learning

Australia • Brazil • Japan • Korea • Mexico • Singapore • Spain • United Kingdom • United States

COURSE TECHNOLOGY
CENGAGE Learning™

Acoustic Design for the Home Studio

Publisher and General Manager:
Stacy L. Hiquet

Associate Director of Marketing:
Sarah O'Donnell

Manager of Editorial Services:
Heather Talbot

Marketing Manager:
Mark Hughes

Executive Editor:
Mike Lawson

Marketing Coordinator:
Meg Dunkerly

Project Editor and Copy Editor:
Cathleen D. Snyder

Editorial Services Coordinator:
Elizabeth Furbish

Cover Designer and Interior Layout Tech:
Stephen Ramirez

Indexer:
Kevin Broccoli

Special thanks to Auralex and RealTraps. Cover: System 5 mixer courtesy Euphonix; studio shots courtesy SoundSound Studio, Cork, Ireland, and Michael Ingvarson, Victoria, Australia.

Important: Course Technology PTR cannot provide software support. Please contact the appropriate software manufacturer's technical support line or Web site for assistance.

Course Technology PTR and the author have attempted throughout this book to distinguish proprietary trademarks from descriptive terms by following the capitalization style used by the manufacturer.

Information contained in this book has been obtained by Course Technology PTR from sources believed to be reliable. However, because of the possibility of human or mechanical error by our sources, Course Technology PTR, or others, the Publisher does not guarantee the accuracy, adequacy, or completeness of any information and is not responsible for any errors or omissions or the results obtained from use of such information. Readers should be particularly aware of the fact that the Internet is an ever-changing entity. Some facts may have changed since this book went to press.

Educational facilities, companies, and organizations interested in multiple copies or licensing of this book should contact the publisher for quantity discount information. Training manuals, CD-ROMs, and portions of this book are also available individually or can be tailored for specific needs.

Library of Congress Catalog Card Number: 2006923268
ISBN 13: 978-1-59863-285-9
ISBN 10: 1-59863-285-X

Course Technology, a division of Cengage Learning
20 Channel Center Street
Boston, MA 02210
www.courseptr.com

Printed in the United States of America
6 7 8 9 10 17 16 15 14 13

This book is dedicated to my mother and father, for all they've done for me over the years.

And to my wonderful (and extremely understanding) wife, Felicia, who makes it all worthwhile.

Foreword

Music, sound, and acoustics go hand in hand…in hand. Well, let's just say that they form a nice, complete circle. Music can be described as an outpouring of creative inspiration and talent expressed through sound vibrations. The late Dick Heyser of the JPL (*Jet Propulsion Labs*) once described sound as "…what happens when air gets pushed."

When sound is created from an instrument, voice, or loudspeaker, these vibrations are transformed and communicated to the listener through the air medium. Unfortunately, once sound has been created, we immediately begin to lose direct control of our musical art through the influences of the room's acoustics. This is the problem that we, as musicians, artists, engineers, and listening enthusiasts, face in creating appropriate acoustics for both the recording and playback environment.

When Mitch Gallagher asked me to review his book, I was extremely pleased to see that it wasn't just a simple rehashing of theoretical acoustical basics or another cookbook of poorly implemented and half-baked solutions. Instead, this is a layman's practical guide to working with a room's acoustics. It focuses on the thinking process of how to approach the acoustics of small production spaces through examples and demonstrated results.

For the purpose of creating the perfect acoustical environment, there are no cookbook solutions that can reliably pertain to every case. Acoustics is an applied science that is part art and part science. That doesn't mean that the "art" part is some form of obscure "black art"; instead, it's a creative application of scientific acoustic principles combined in a way that produces the desired environment.

If you build four walls and a roof in which to create, manipulate, and listen to sound, you've committed acoustics. Your sound is now at the mercy of other forces at play in both the studio where it is performed and then again in the listening/mixing environment where it is reproduced. The question is how to best approach the task of taming our acoustical environment.

With *Acoustic Design for the Home Studio*, Mitch has succeeded in making the application of this perceptual science of acoustics for the personal production space more understandable, relevant, and fun.

—Russ Berger, Russ Berger Design Group

Acknowledgments

A book like this is so much more than the work of just one person. Some of those who gave freely to this project include Tracy Chandler at Auralex Acoustics, John Storyk at Walters-Storyk Design Group, Peter Janis at Primacoustic, Ethan Winer at RealTraps, Andrea Rotondo and Steve Wilson, Mike Lawson, and Cathleen Snyder, Heather Talbot, Elizabeth Furbish, and Stacy Hiquet at Thomson Course Technology PTR.

David Stewart took many of the photos in this book (he took the good ones; the bad ones are mine, though he did his Photoshop best to make those presentable as well). Thanks David! And thanks to Liane Stewart for moving the phone line….

Russ Berger at Russ Berger Design Group provided generous advice and technical information, and gave even more generously of his time and creativity to contribute the fantasy studio in Chapter 11. (I only wish I had the funds to build it!) Plus he contributed the Foreword to this book. I am very grateful.

Jeff Szymanski at Auralex Acoustics went *way* beyond the call of duty for this project. Not only did he serve as a sounding board for ideas, a source of endless advice and information, and a wonderful volunteer technical editor, he also performed all the room analysis and provided all the room response graphs in this book. Mere thanks are not enough to express my appreciation.

And most of all, thanks to my wife, Felicia, for her endless enthusiasm, support, and love during this project.

About the Author

Mitch Gallagher hails originally from Jamestown, North Dakota, the home of the world's largest buffalo. He was introduced to recording music when the manager of the rock band he was in loaned the group a four-track cassette recorder. His background includes studies in electrical engineering and computer science, and a bachelor's degree in music from Moorhead State University in Moorhead, Minnesota (now known as Minnesota State University, Moorhead). Graduate studies in composition, electronic music composition, and classical guitar took him to the University of Missouri, Kansas City.

As a guitarist, he toured the Midwest for several years playing rock and country music. He has performed with big bands, jazz-rock fusion groups, experimental music groups, in small ensembles, and as a classical and steel-string guitar soloist. He has taught countless guitar lessons, both private and in university classrooms.

As a composer, he has worked in both the commercial and classical realms. *Prophecy #1: At First Glance,* his experimental work for percussion ensemble and synthesizers, received a NARAS (Grammy) award.

He began building his first project studio with a Commodore 64 computer, primitive MIDI software, a low-end drum machine, and a small Radio Shack PA for monitoring. Eventually his studio evolved into MAG Media Productions, which provides a full range of recording, mixing, editing, mastering, and production services, as well as freelance writing and editing services.

In addition to years spent in pro audio retail and as a freelance recording and live sound engineer, Gallagher has taught university-level recording and electronic music classes and labs, and many seminars on recording, MIDI, and live sound. He has lectured on music technology topics throughout the United States and in Europe.

Gallagher was named Senior Technical Editor of *Keyboard* magazine in 1998. In January 2000, Gallagher assumed the editor in chief's chair at *EQ* magazine and remained in that post for five years. He has published nearly 1,000 product reviews and articles on music technology and recording in magazines such as *Performing Songwriter, EQ, Keyboard, Pro Sound News, Guitar Player, Government Video, Extreme Groove, Music Technology Buyer's Guide, Videography,* and *Microphones & Monitors,* as well as in magazines in Japan, Australia, and throughout Europe. His first book, *Make Music Now!* (Backbeat Books), was released in 2002. His second, *Pro Tools Clinic: Demystifying LE for Macintosh and PC* (Schirmer Trade Books, 2004) was named the top-selling instructional book by *Music & Sound Retailer* magazine.

Contents

Introduction

Way back in the early 1980s, while I was in college, I built my first "recording studio"–a used Commodore 64 computer (64k of RAM, yow!) running a primitive MIDI sequencer, a cheap drum machine, some guitars run through a Sholz Rockman, and the JVC cassette deck from my stereo. Okay, "built" may be a bit strong; I set my gear on a shelf in my small bedroom and listened over headphones. Over the years that studio inexorably expanded; I'd save up a few bucks or break out the credit cards and pick up some new "toys." The gear kept getting better and better, and my skills improved as I studied and worked on recording techniques and gained experience in the studio.

But over the past few years, I've come to the same realization as many other home and project studio owners: The equipment we have is capable of excellent—even professional—results, assuming we have the skill to use it properly. With the technology we have available today, even the least expensive recording equipment is capable of producing outstanding audio quality compared to just a few short years ago.

But despite that fact, there's nonetheless clearly been a limitation on our home studios. The gear has gotten much better, and we've learned a great deal about recording. So why do so many musicians and engineers have difficulty getting truly "pro"-sounding results? We've found that more gear doesn't always solve the problem. More study and practice will definitely make a difference, but it still seems much harder to get great results at home than in a "commercial" or professional room.

One reason? Acoustics. If the room you're working in doesn't sound good, and if it's not "accurate," then it will be extremely difficult—if not impossible—to produce excellent-sounding results. You can't capture a true sound if the mics aren't hearing the instruments and vocals correctly. You have to be able to hear what's truly going on with your tracks to make the proper decisions about editing, equalizing, processing, and mixing them. And even if you have the best studio monitor speakers in the world, if your room sounds bad or isn't even in its response, then you're not hearing what's really going on with the music.

Acoustics can be a complex, math-laden science, but treating a room to make it sound great and to function optimally as a recording studio needn't be difficult nor require hours in front of a calculator or computer screen. Understanding a few basic principles and how to apply them to acoustic treatments can take you a long way toward having a studio that sounds accurate. We may never have a room at home that can match the best professionally designed commercial studio (at least not without dumping in a pile of cash and a *lot* of effort), but we can get a long way in that direction without major construction and without spending much money.

That's where this book comes in. In these pages you'll learn the basic principles of acoustics that affect you in your home or project studio, and how to solve any acoustic problems you may have without laying out much (or any) money. Whether you're converting a bedroom, a garage, a basement, or a corner of the living room, this book will help you improve the sound of the environment in which you're making music.

The principles are easy to understand, and the materials used for treating a room are easy enough to find and work with. Whether you want to pursue a "no-cost" solution, use "off-the-shelf" acoustic materials, or even if you have an unlimited budget, we'll look at how to put your room together easily and effectively.

In my current studio and in my previous studio—both located in my home and put together in such a way that there was no construction required or permanent damage to the rooms—I was able to create reference-quality recording and mixing environments using the techniques and materials discussed in this book. It's not difficult; two friends and I treated my current studio, including a recording booth and main/control room, in just a few hours (not counting the pizza break) using off-the-shelf materials—and the results have been excellent.

Read on! With some thought, a little work, and a small investment in materials, your studio can become the stellar recording retreat you've always wanted. Your tracks will sound better, it will be easier to achieve the results you're after, and making music will be even more fun!

Part I

Acoustics and Sound Control

CHAPTER 1

Acoustics Defined

Let's begin with a definition (taken from the Microsoft Word dictionary, but similar definitions are found in *Merriam-Webster Online* and other dictionaries):

---

a·cous·tics. ***noun***. 1. The scientific study of sound. 2. The characteristic way in which sound carries or can be heard within a particular enclosed space, for example, an auditorium.

In other words, acoustics deals with what sound does in a room. "But wait," I hear you say, "I'm a recording engineer [feel free to substitute "musician," "songwriter," "producer," or "composer" as is appropriate for what you do]; what do I care about scientifically studying sound or what it does in a room? It's the music that matters to me!"

That's certainly a valid response. What matters most *is* the music—and making the music sound its best. For those of us into recording, "making the music sound its best" usually takes the form of obsessing over getting the best gear we can afford and getting the best possible quality from that gear. Visit a newsstand and look over the pro audio magazines—*Mix*, *Sound On Sound*, *Tape Op*, and others. You'll find their pages packed with gear reviews and how-to articles. Fire up your browser and cruise the Net. You'll encounter dozens of online forums filled to bursting with topics such as "Which preamp should I buy?" "Which microphone is best for acoustic guitar?" "Which monitor speakers are most accurate?" "How can I get the best vocal recording?" "How should I mike my kick drum for the best sound?"

There's nothing wrong with that; discussing gear and how to use it can be very educational, and will almost certainly result in better recordings (and it's fun). But by immersing ourselves in this non-stop search for the best gear, we often ignore the one thing that can have the biggest impact on our recordings and mixes: the acoustics of the rooms we're working in. Yes, a sexy new tube preamp may make a noticeable improvement in your tracks (plus it will look *really cool* in your rack). But taming problematic acoustics in your recording space and control room will likely make a much bigger difference in the quality of the recordings you make. In fact, in most cases, improving the acoustics of your room will result in the biggest sonic improvement you're going to get.

When the room sounds its best, microphones can accurately capture sound sources, unaffected by problem acoustics. Monitors can play back as accurately as they're able, without interference from the room's problematic characteristics. When a room sounds and "feels" good, musicians perform better. Most important of all, you'll be able to accurately *hear* what's happening with your music. And that's what it's all about—being able to hear your music well enough to make rational decisions about quality, tonality, and performances. When the room is accurate, the music you produce there will translate well on other people's stereos, in cars, on MP3 players, over the radio or TV, in the theater—it will sound the way it's supposed to sound no matter where it's played.

Commercial studios spend thousands and thousands (and thousands) of dollars hiring professional studio designers and highly credentialed acousticians to design and build acoustically optimized spaces—and the results are worth it. Unfortunately, most of us working in home and project studios don't have the budget to hire a pro or to make the sort of structural changes required for world-class sound. But that doesn't mean that we can't vastly improve the sound of the rooms and spaces we use for recording and mixing. For surprisingly little money, we can make even the worst acoustical situation much better. And in most cases, by investing a small amount of money (and a fair amount of sweat equity) we can create very good-sounding—even great-sounding—spaces in which to make and record music.

Acoustics versus Sound Isolation

There tends to be a great deal of confusion over what we're talking about when we discuss acoustic treatment for studios; we're not talking about stopping your screaming 100-watt Marshall amp from annoying your entire apartment building. Nor are we stopping sound so that the neighbors don't call the police every time your band rehearses. Both of those are examples of "isolation"—

stopping the transmission of sound from one location to another. We'll talk about some isolation and noise control techniques later in this book—though true soundproofing generally requires construction beyond the scope of this tome. (Those in the acoustics "business" tend to discourage the use of the term "soundproof," equating it to calling a watch "waterproof.") Rather, most of our attention will be focused on acoustics—per our definition at the beginning of this chapter, the way in which sound behaves *within* a room. Our goal is to use various materials to treat the acoustics within our rooms so that the sound behaves in a controlled, predictable, and non-destructive manner. There's almost no overlap between the two concepts; most acoustical treatment material will have little or no sound isolation value, and vice versa. In fact, in some cases, extensive soundproofing can make the acoustics within a room *worse* than they were before.

Basics of Sound

The first step in getting the acoustics in your space under control is gaining a bit of an understanding of sound itself.

SOUND WAVES AND FREQUENCY

Sound travels in waves (which scientists have cleverly decided to call "sound waves")—similar to the waves you see in a lake or in the ocean. Vibration of a sound source creates wave motion in the air. The *frequency*, or how fast the wave vibrates, determines the *pitch* of the sound. A common example is "*A*-440," often used as a tuning reference for instruments. Basically, *A*-440 means that the note *A* has a frequency of 440 Hz, which means 440 cycles, or wave vibrations, per second. ("Hz" stands for "hertz," named for Heinrich Hertz, a late-19th-century physicist who figured this stuff out. Hertz's *Principles of Mechanics* was groundbreaking in its day, and is still a valued reference.) The higher the note, the higher the frequency. A low note on a bass guitar might be at 45 Hz. Something like the shimmer on a crash cymbal might have a much higher frequency, up in the 6,000, 7,000, or even 10,000 Hz range. (Large numbers like these are generally represented by "kilohertz," or "kHz." A kilohertz is a thousand hertz, so 6,000 Hz is written as 6 kHz, 10,000 Hz is abbreviated 10 kHz, 7,500 Hz becomes 7.5 kHz, and so on.) Doubling the frequency of a note moves it up an octave in musical terms. So an *A* at 880 Hz is an octave above *A*-440.

Figure 1.1
Here we see two tones, one at 20 Hz, the other at 40 Hz. Note that the wave cycles for the 40 Hz tone occur twice as fast—it has double the frequency of the 20 Hz tone. In musical terms it sounds one octave higher.

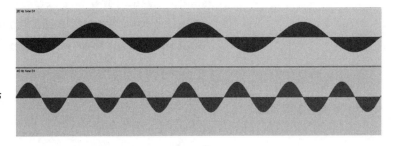

Human hearing is generally accepted to extend from around 20 Hz to 20 kHz. However, the range of frequencies extends from 0 Hz up to hundreds of thousands of cycles per second, and beyond, even though most people can't hear to those extremes! For acoustic treatment of home and project studios—or any studios for that matter—we're generally most concerned with the frequencies that fall in the human range of hearing and lower.

A related aspect is *frequency response*, or how a piece of gear (or a room) responds to the range of frequencies.

Ideally, response would be the same at every frequency (called "flat response"), and with electronic audio equipment, certain pieces of gear can get close. But with rooms, flat response is virtually impossible. Still, one of our goals as we treat our studios will be to make the frequency response as even and flat as possible. In fact, really all we're able to accomplish—even with extensive treatment—is to reduce the worst response problems and smooth things out a bit. But that's good enough for our ears; with reasonably even response, our hearing has enough power to compensate for the response anomalies that remain.

AMPLITUDE

The volume or "level" of a sound is measured using *decibels*, or "dB," named for Alexander Graham Bell. A decibel is often defined as the smallest volume change that the human ear can perceive without a reference to compare against, in isolation. (But with another sound to reference, trained ears can often hear changes as small as 1/10th of a decibel.)

Not to get all mathematical on you, but because the range of sound levels our ears can perceive is so wide, the decibel scale is logarithmic to keep things manageable. A very quiet professional recording studio might have 30 to 40 dB in background noise, whereas getting up close and personal with a jet airplane engine might measure 140 dB. Comfortable music listening (except for those into heavy metal) might be in the 70–90 dB range, while a rock concert often hits 120–130 dB.

What this logarithmic scale means for us is that you don't need to make much of a change dB-wise to hear a relatively large change in the volume or tone of a signal; 3 dB of increase or decrease is quite a bit, and 10 dB is doubling of loudness.

WAVELENGTH

Here's a big surprise: The measurement of a sound wave's physical length is called its *wavelength*. Wavelength is related to the frequency of the wave; the higher the frequency, the shorter the wavelength, and the lower the frequency, the longer the wavelength. This measurement is important when you're dealing with acoustics because wavelength, in combination with phase (see the next section, "Phase"), affects where there will be problems in a room.

Table 1.1 Frequency versus Wavelength	
Frequency	**Wavelength**
20 Hz	56.3 feet
60 Hz	18.8 feet
100 Hz	11.3 feet
160 Hz	7.0 feet
320 Hz	3.5 feet
500 Hz	2.3 feet
1 kHz	1.1 feet
2.5 kHz	5.4 inches
5 kHz	2.7 inches
10 kHz	1.4 inches
20 kHz	0.7 inches

PHASE

The term *phase* describes the relationship of two waves or signals in time. Each wave is continually passing through its 360-degree cycle of peak and trough; if two identical waves that are at different points in their cycles are combined, problems can occur.

Figure 1.2
A sound wave travels in a continuous series of peaks and troughs whose progress is measured in degrees.

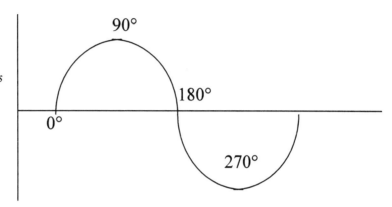

Phase is extremely important in acoustics (and in recording in general) because waves that are out of phase by even a small amount can cancel each other, resulting in tonal changes.

Figure 1.3
These two waveforms are 180° out of phase. If they are combined, they will cancel each other out completely, resulting in silence. But cancellation can occur if waves are as little as 1° out of phase, producing a "hollow," thin sound with reduced volume.

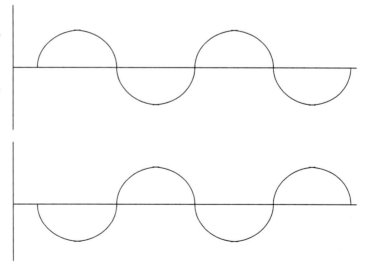

Likewise, waves that are in phase reinforce each other, making the signal stronger. Phase problems occur when sound bounces around within a room; the reflecting waves interfere with each other destructively, causing all sorts of problems. We'll be talking a lot more about this starting with the next chapter.

CHAPTER 2

Reflection Control

Mathematics and physics aside—not that those two things can be easily cast aside when you're discussing acoustics—the behavior of sound in rooms at the "10,000-foot view" is conceptually pretty easy to understand. A sound wave can be reflected by the surfaces in the room and bounce around, it can be partially absorbed and bounce around a bit less, or it can pass through or around the surfaces in the room and exit to the outside.

Any of these behaviors can be problematic for a studio—sound waves bouncing around inside a room can interfere with one another, which makes mixing and recording in the room difficult, and sound waves that escape from the room can interfere with your good relationship with your family and neighbors! Plus, if sound waves are getting out of your room, you can bet there's potential for stray noise to get into the room from the outside as well. We'll be discussing the behavior of sound inside the room in this chapter; sound isolation to prevent sound leaking in and out of the room will be covered in Chapter 13, "Sound Isolation."

Sound in a Room

How sound behaves inside a room depends on a number of factors—the frequency of the sound wave; the shape and dimensions of the room; the materials that the walls, ceiling, and floor are made of and covered with; how many doors and windows there are and where they're placed; and the contents of the room (furniture, tapestries, equipment, musicians, lava lamps). We'll cover those factors as we work our way through the next few chapters.

One of the biggest factors that determines what happens with sound in a room is the frequency of the sound wave. At lower frequencies, wavelengths are long, and sound waves have a tendency to bend around objects in the room to pass through lighter materials and to spread out in an omnidirectional (every direction at once) pattern; we'll be talking a lot more about how low frequencies behave in a room in the next chapter.

At mid and high frequencies—say, 100 Hz or so and above—sound waves are quite predictable in their behavior: They're directional (like the beam of a flashlight), bounce off hard surfaces, and are absorbed by softer materials. It works very much like a rubber ball being bounced. Throw the ball against a hard surface such as a concrete floor or a plaster wall, and it will bounce right off at an angle that corresponds to the angle at which it was thrown against the surface. (To be technically correct, a surface has to have a dimension equal to a wavelength to reflect sound in this manner. So our 100 Hz wave will bounce off a roughly 12-foot-wide wall, but will diffract around objects that have no dimension that large.)

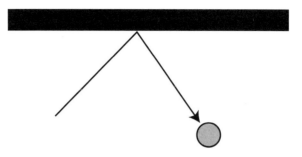

Figure 2.1
Sound inside a room bounces off surfaces just like a ball thrown against a hard wall.

Add a corner to the equation, and the ball will bounce its way off both surfaces.

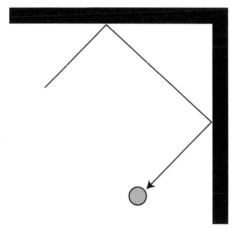

Figure 2.2
More surfaces mean more bouncing, whether you're talking about balls or sound waves.

However, throw the ball against a soft surface such as a pillow, and it will either stop dead and fall to the ground or bounce off with much-reduced velocity. It works much the same with mid- and high-frequency sound waves. They bounce off hard surfaces and are absorbed, to one extent or another, by "softer" materials. How much absorption occurs depends on the material the surface is made of and covered with.

That's the basic idea, but with sound waves, things are more complex than they are with a rubber ball. First of all, sound waves generated by an instrument, vocalist, or studio monitor speaker are dispersed in multiple directions simultaneously, not just along one path like a thrown ball. (In fact, most monitors will have a "dispersion" specification that defines how sound spreads out from the speaker drivers.)

Figure 2.3
Sound leaving a loudspeaker disperses in many directions simultaneously.

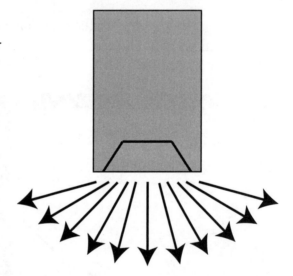

The second factor is the listener (you). If you're positioned in front of the speaker, you'll hear sound waves coming at you directly from the speaker. But you'll also hear other sound waves reflected off nearby walls and other surfaces.

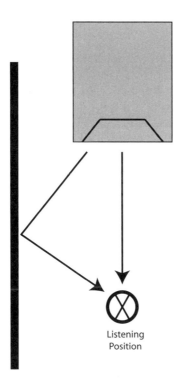

Figure 2.4
If you're in front of a speaker,
you'll hear direct sound as
well as sound reflected from
surfaces around you.

Listening
Position

The problem is that you hear the sounds directly from the speaker a very short time before you hear the sound reflected off the wall—how long the delay is depends on how far away the nearest surface is that reflects sound back to you.

This time delay or difference in arrival time between the two waves can result in—remember our discussion back in Chapter 1—phase differences in the waves. As the direct waves and the reflected waves combine, the time/phase delay can cause cancellations and reinforcements in the sound waves, changing the tonality of what you're hearing. (This effect is known as *comb filtering.*) And if the tonality is changed, you're not hearing what's really there, coming out of the speaker.

First Reflections

The worst culprits in the reflected sound game are the *first reflections*—sound waves that come back to your ears after one bounce, less than 20 milliseconds or so after the direct sound. Sound travels at a rate of about one foot per millisecond, so that means that any reflective surface within about 10 feet or so of the listening position (making the round trip the reflected sound wave makes from speaker to wall to your ears about 20 feet) will cause problems. This includes walls to the side or behind, the ceiling, equipment racks, mixing console—any reflective surface.

But fear not; this doesn't mean that you have to be 10 feet away from any reflective surface in order to be able to record or mix well. There are things we can do to reduce or eliminate first reflections so that smaller rooms will work just fine. We'll get to them later in this chapter.

Flutter Echo

There can be another problem with upper-mid and high-frequency sound waves bouncing around in a room. If waves are reflected directly between two parallel surfaces—say, opposing walls in a small room—you'll often hear a rattling sound, a fast echo effect known as *flutter echo*. Check it out yourself; walk into a smallish room with hard, parallel bare walls and clap your hands. You'll hear the characteristic fast echo between the walls. Monitor speakers or any other sound source positioned between bare, hard walls can cause the same effect.

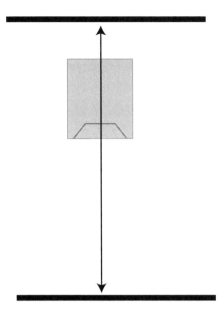

Figure 2.5
Flutter echo is caused by sound reflecting back and forth between parallel hard surfaces (such as walls).

Not only can flutter echo be a problem when you are sitting in front of your monitor speakers, but it can be a real problem when you're using a microphone to record an instrument. Fortunately, as with first reflections, flutter echo can be dealt with pretty easily—in fact, the same treatments often help with both problems.

Reverberant Decay

Once the sound in your room gets past the first reflection stage, the remaining reflected sound will tend to wash together, creating *reverberation*—the sound left ringing in the room after the direct sound from the speaker or sound source stops. (For an extreme example of reverberation, think of the long wash of echo-y sound in a large gymnasium, church, or auditorium after you clap your hands or shout.)

For most recording and mixing tasks, too much reverberation, or reverberation that lasts too long, is a problem—it's hard to hear clearly through a wash of ringing sound that carries on long after the direct sound has stopped. Clarity will be compromised, and there may be phase problems. If you are recording multiple instruments, each in the same room with too much reverb in it, when you mix those tracks together, the combined reverb will be overwhelming.

The amount of time it takes for the reverberation in a room to drop in level by 60 decibels is known as *RT60*. However, small rooms (including many control rooms, studios, and recording booths) aren't large enough to develop a statistically significant reverberation field that can be quantified by the RT60 measurement standards and techniques. That isn't to say there's no reverberant energy in the room. Rather, it means that in many small rooms, RT60 is the wrong metric for measuring and characterizing reverberant decay.

Controlling the reverberant decay for a room is very important for ensuring good response. Equally important is making sure that the reverberant decay across the frequency range is even. If the reverberant decay for high frequencies is different than for low frequencies, the room will have a characteristic sound that probably won't be desirable—a bright ring, boomy low end, or uneven midrange. However, if the reverberant decay is too short, the room will have a dry, dead feeling and sound that will be uncomfortable for musicians and vocalists and may cause you to add too much artificial ambience and reverberation to your mixes.

Controlling Reflections and Reverberation

So assuming we're faced with an empty room with hard surfaces on the walls, ceiling, and floor, how do we control reflections and reverberant decay? There are two different methods, each of which is effective for solving certain problems; the two also overlap in their results to an extent. These two methods are absorption and diffusion. Some studio designers prefer using absorption, others use diffusion, and still others like to use a combination of the two.

ABSORPTION

For smaller studios and home and project studios, absorption tends to be the primary method for controlling mid- and high-frequency first reflections, flutter echo, and reverberant decay. The idea is to use soft materials placed at the main reflection points to reduce—absorb—sonic energy so that the level of the reflected sound waves is significantly quieter than the direct sound from the speakers. In fact, what happens is that as the sound wave passes through the absorptive material, its energy is converted to heat.

Figure 2.6
Sound waves pass through the absorptive material and are reflected back. But in passing through the material in two directions (going and coming), a certain amount of the sound energy is converted to heat. This results in the reflected sound being quieter, and therefore much less destructive.

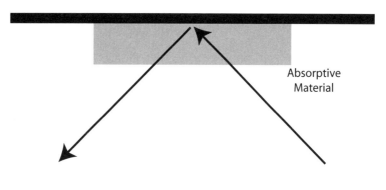

Absorptive
Material

Absorption works best with midrange and high frequencies. Lower frequencies require large quantities of absorptive material for effective energy reduction, so they're treated somewhat differently. (We'll discuss this in detail in the next chapter.)

High frequencies have very little energy compared to low frequencies, so thin, soft materials can be used to absorb them. As the frequency gets lower, thicker and thicker absorptive materials are required—and as a side benefit, those thicker materials are even more effective at controlling higher frequencies.

So what sorts of materials work? Several companies manufacture acoustic foam that is designed specifically for absorbing midrange and high-frequency sound waves. Don't confuse these types of acoustic foam—known as *open cell* foam—with various types of packing foam or similar materials. There is a *major* difference in how effectively foam designed for sound absorption works for controlling reflections compared to foam designed to fill a packing crate! The other difference is that acoustic foam is generally rated as flame retardant—an important factor because some types of foam are extremely flammable, and therefore not safe for residences and businesses.

Glass fiber is another common absorptive material. The rigid variety, such as Owens-Corning 700 Fiberglass™ series, is fairly easy to work with, but there are also uses for fluffier varieties. Glass fiber, of course, can be a major irritant, so you have to cover it to prevent strands from getting into the air.

Other soft materials will also absorb mid and high frequencies. Pillows, curtains and drapes, blankets, carpet, furniture, and so on all absorb sound to one degree or another. We'll be discussing the use of some of these materials in upcoming chapters.

TOO MUCH OF A GOOD THING?

Absorption seems easy enough to use. You just line the walls, floor, and ceiling of your studio with sound-absorbing material and start making noise!

But it's not quite that simple. Many types of absorptive materials only work well on higher frequencies, leaving midrange sound bouncing around without much control. This can result in an odd, dark-sounding room with no high end. There will be too much absorption in the upper frequencies, so the mids and highs will be reduced while the bass frequencies will be running around with abandon, resulting in a boomy, bassy room that sounds muddy.

Overdo the overall absorption, and the room will be too dead—it will be uncomfortable to work in. In my experience, most rooms require less absorption than we initially think; the idea is to use just enough to control first reflections and to tame reverberant decay. Keep in mind that you can always add more absorption if the room still seems too live or first reflections aren't reduced enough.

The first key to finding the right amount of absorption is balance—enough absorption to control the mids and highs, and enough bass control to end up with a balanced room response and an even reverberant decay across the frequency range. The second key is placing the absorptive materials in the proper locations so they will be as effective as possible.

DIFFUSION

Where absorption uses various materials to absorb the sound wave's energy and thus lower its level, *diffusion* scatters the sound wave, breaking a single reflection up into many smaller reflections going out in many different directions. Because there are no "big" reflections going back to the listener, first reflection problems are reduced, and because diffusive materials are irregular in shape, flutter echo is eliminated. While reverberation won't be eliminated, scattering and breaking up the reflections tends to result in a smoother reverberation at a lower level.

Figure 2.7
Diffusion breaks up a sound wave into smaller waves that are scattered in many directions.

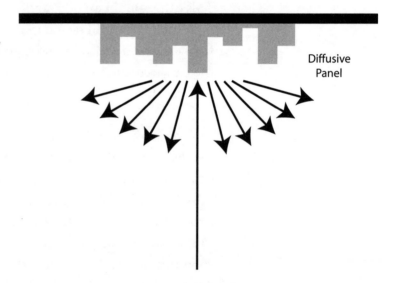

Diffusive Panel

While any irregular surface will break up reflections at some frequencies to a degree, scientific, or calculated, diffusion that evenly scatters a broad frequency range of sound waves requires specialized diffusion materials. Such scientific diffusors can be difficult to build or make on your own, and commercially available units can be somewhat pricy. There are some affordable off-the-shelf diffusors, which work well on higher frequencies. And other materials can be used, though their effectiveness won't be as great nor will they affect as broad a range of frequencies.

For most home and project studios, our focus will primarily be on absorption, but diffusion will play a role as well. We'll look at some diffusion techniques and materials in Chapter 5, "Acoustic Treatments."

CHAPTER 3

The Low-Down

Dealing with midrange and high frequencies is relatively simple; it's not hard to figure out where those sound waves are going and how to control them. (We'll learn how shortly.) Low frequencies are an entirely different proposition.

Most recording engineers would agree that low frequencies cause more problems than mid or high frequencies. It's almost impossible to get the bass to "sit" right in a mix if the room has low-frequency problems; you may add too much low end to a track or mix because you're hearing too little bass, or vice versa — you may think you have enough bottom, but because the room is boomy and muddy, you don't actually have enough low end. What happens is that your mixes don't translate. When you play them in your studio, they sound fine, but take them to your car, play them at your friend's house on her stereo, or load them in an iPod, and things just don't sound right.

Even worse, bass response can vary dramatically in different locations in the room—moving as little as a few inches may result in a completely different bass response. And it's not unusual to have variations in low frequency response that run to 15, 20, or even 30 dB or more. Furthermore, those variations can occur within just a few cycles per second of one another.

Sounds pretty bad, doesn't it? Fear not. Once we understand what causes low-frequency problems in a room, we can figure out what we need to do to correct the problems.

Room Modes and Standing Waves

Inside a room, low-frequency sound waves reflect between walls and create *standing waves*—a.k.a., "room modes," "modes of vibration," "resonant modes," or simply *modes*. (*Note*: To be semantically accurate, standing waves aren't necessarily modes, though all modes are standing waves. The reasons are somewhat tweaky and won't affect how we treat our rooms.)

A room mode creates resonance, or boost in a particular frequency. In addition, a mode results in a longer reverb decay time at that frequency, which some current research is proving to be even more problematic for monitoring and recording than a simple level boost. But the problem doesn't stop there. There will also be level boosts at frequencies occurring at octaves above the mode. So if there is a mode at 50 Hz, there will also be problems at 100 Hz, 150 Hz, 200 Hz, and so on. In fact, the modes continue up above the "low frequency" range, all the way through the audio range. But above 200 to 300 Hz, the modes tend to get so closely packed together that the effect is almost uniform; the effects of comb filtering and cancellation at higher frequencies is far more evident than resonances from room modes.

A room's modes are determined by its three dimensions: length, width, and height. As we saw earlier, each mode creates problems at octaves above as well. So with three dimensions to consider, you can see that the low-frequency response of a room can get very complex, very quickly. In Figure 3.1, we see the low-frequency response curve for the small recording booth in the author's studio. The arrows indicate how the calculated room modes line up with the peaks and dips in the room's measured frequency response.

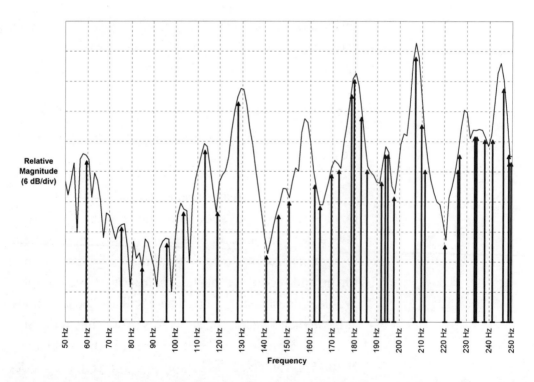

Figure 3.1: Talk about complex; look at how many modes a room that measures 114 inches long by 80 inches wide by 90 inches high creates under 250 Hz! (Courtesy of Auralex Acoustics, Inc.)

No matter how big or small your room is, it will have modes—there's simply no way to eliminate them. But a small room typically has bigger problems because of the way in which the modes are spaced. You can minimize the problems room modes cause by increasing dimensions—longer dimensions result in lower modes. You can also space the modes "better" by making sure the room's three dimensions aren't related. We'll talk more about room dimensions in the next chapter.

Unfortunately, changing dimensions isn't very easy to do if you're working with a room that's already finished—which is the case in almost all home and project studios, unless you're doing heavy remodeling and major rebuilding, or can somehow couple the volume of adjacent spaces.

Three Types of Modes

There are actually three types of modes that occur within virtually every room:

▶ **Axial modes.** The sound wave reflects between two parallel surfaces.

▶ **Tangential modes.** The sound wave bounces across four surfaces.

▶ **Oblique modes.** The sound wave travels across all six surfaces of a room.

Axial modes are the biggest problem where modes are concerned, with tangential modes coming in as somewhat secondary. In most cases, oblique modes aren't a significant problem because they tend to occur at higher frequencies and decay in level quickly. In most cases you can ignore them—unless your room is made of solid concrete on all six surfaces!

WHY BASS VARIES AROUND A ROOM

With all those modes flying around the room, there are going to be a lot of places where sound waves boost one another and where they destructively interfere, or cancel, each other. This means that there is a spatial factor to the room's modal response. In other words, where your speakers are placed in the room, and where you're listening from will make a big difference in the low end that you are hearing. It's easy to prove it: Just play low frequency tones and walk around; listen near walls, in the corner, in the front, in the middle, and in the back in the room. Unless you have an acoustically magical room, you'll clearly hear the bass varying from place to place. The graph in Figure 3.2 shows the low-frequency response for the recording booth we looked at earlier. In this case, we see the response measured at three different physical positions in the booth. The first is the response with the mic placed where it would be when recording a standing vocalist. Next is with the mic placed where it would be when recording a guitar amp driving a 4×12 speaker cabinet—near to the floor and about a foot back from the speaker. Finally, we see the response with the mic placed where it would be when recording a steel-string acoustic guitar—the mic is placed as if it were looking at the 14th fret of the guitar.

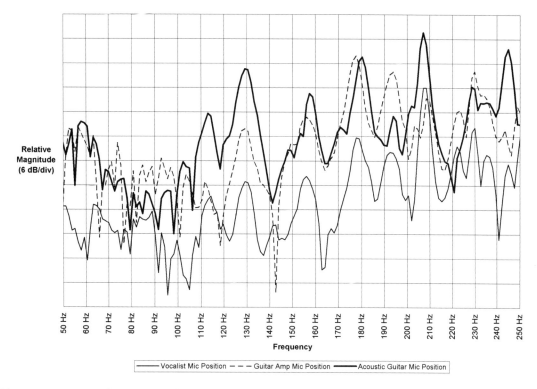

Relative
Magnitude
(6 dB/div)

Frequency

—— Vocalist Mic Position — — — Guitar Amp Mic Position ——— Acoustic Guitar Mic Position

Figure 3.2 At some frequencies the difference in response among the positions is as much as 27 decibels! (Courtesy of Auralex Acoustics, Inc.)

Low end also tends to "build up" in corners and near walls. For this reason you should never place a monitor speaker in or near a corner if you can help it, and it's best to place your monitors away from nearby walls if possible. In Figure 3.3, you can see that in the "control room" area of the author's untreated studio, low-frequency response measurements were taken at the engineer's listening position (in the "sweet spot"); at the producer's listening position, which is behind the engineer a few feet; and against the rear wall of the room. The circle on the graph shows the buildup of certain frequencies against the wall.

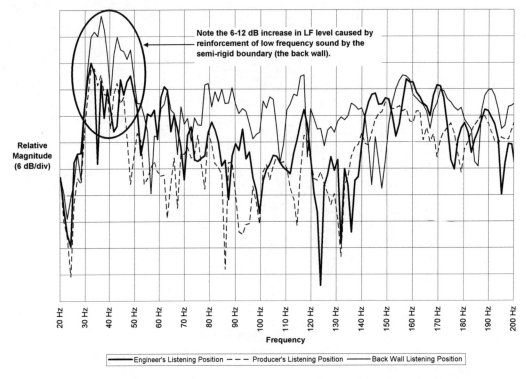

Figure 3.3: Low-frequency response measurements were taken at three places in the room. (Courtesy of Auralex Acoustics, Inc.)

The goal of treating a room acoustically is to minimize the dips and peaks in a room's response, as well as to even out the reverb decay of the various frequencies. It's pretty much impossible to completely flatten out the response; the best we can hope for with careful treatment is to reduce peaks and dips to within a range of ±6 to ±10 dB or so. But that's *well* within the "good enough" range where our ears can adjust and perceive what's happening just fine.

This all works because even though modes result in different boosts and dips in various places in the room, by treating one location in a mode, you'll also treat all the rest—the boosts and dips are "symptoms" of the problem. Treat the root of the problem—the mode itself—and all the symptoms will be treated as well.

BASS TRAPPING

If you have a perfectly rectangular room—no niches, alcoves, cutouts, or other irregularities—it's fairly easy to figure out where the modes will occur. The formula is simple: The fundamental frequency of the mode (F) equals the speed of sound (1,130 feet per second, or 343 meters per second) divided by twice the room dimension you're concerned about (D).

$$F = 1,130/2D$$

So if the width of your room is 10 feet, a mode will occur at 56.5 Hz (1,130/20). Keep in mind that there will also be modes at 113 Hz, 169.5 Hz, 226 Hz, and so on—at the "harmonics" above the fundamental modal frequency.

Unfortunately, if your room deviates from a perfect rectangle in any dimension, calculating its modes will be much more difficult. Fortunately, depending on what treatment you're using, it may not be really necessary to know exactly what the modes are in your room in order to treat the low-frequency response.

A room's low-frequency response can be shaped using what are called *bass traps*. There are two types of traps; the first are *tuned absorbers*. There are two different types. Slatted or *Helmholtz* devices—which function as resonators (think of blowing across the top of a soda bottle)—and panel or membrane traps, where a "membrane" (say, a thin sheet of wood) vibrates in response to low frequencies. Both resonator and membrane traps are designed and built to solve problems occurring at specific frequencies. It's possible to play with the design a bit to get broader response, but in general, tuned absorbers are, well, *tuned* to a particular frequency. Designed and installed correctly, these traps can be very effective. But figuring out the proper traps generally takes some doing, and building them can be challenging if you aren't skilled with woodworking. While there are commercial tuned absorbers available, they tend to be expensive, and it's always questionable how well they will work in your particular room unless you *really* have the modal frequencies figured out.

The second type of bass trap is far more common in home and project rooms—broadband absorbers, which are technically called "porous" absorbers because the air motion of the sound wave is allowed to flow into the absorptive material, where it is converted to heat. Porous absorbers are simply large, thick absorbers that are placed in appropriate locations and control a wide range of frequencies. Broadband absorbers have the benefit of covering a wider range of frequencies at the same time; many even help with mid- and high-frequency problems. The disadvantage is that for very low-frequency control, these absorbers need to be quite large. But back on the positive side, broadband absorbers are easy to build and install, and there are some off-the-shelf models available that aren't too pricey.

We're going to talk a lot more about bass traps in Chapter 5, "Acoustic Treatments."

CAN YOU TRAP TOO MUCH?

So is it possible to put too many bass traps in a room and suck all the low end out? Probably not. Even if you treat all the wall-to-wall corners, wall-to-ceiling corners, and wall-to-floor corners, as well as all the junctions of two walls and the ceiling, you probably won't have overdone the bass trapping in a small room. However, if you're using glass fiber panels across the corners or foam bass traps, you may have added too much high-frequency absorption in the room. In that case, using glass fiber panels with metallic facing on one side will help restore some high end.

CHAPTER 4

The Good, the Bad, and the Ugly

Unfortunately, not all rooms are created equal when it comes to good sound. The size and volume of the room make a big difference, the shape has a big effect, and the ratios of the three room dimensions have a major impact.

Unfortunately, most of us don't have control over the room dimensions we have available to us in our studios—usually the choice of a studio room comes down to which bedroom is least used, where there's space in the basement, whether you can park your car in the driveway since you've converted the garage…in other words, wherever your husband or wife will tolerate.

Still, it doesn't hurt to understand a bit about why certain rooms might work better than others. Besides, someday you may be able to build a studio building in the back yard, and after reading this, you'll be set….

Room Dimensions

· ·

While room dimensions certainly aren't the be-all and end-all of studio design, there are some "rules" of thumb that result in a good starting point for a studio or recording space.

1. The worst possible room dimensions result in a perfect cube, such as 10 feet long by 10 feet wide by 10 feet high. The reason? All three dimensions will result in the exact same modes—ouch! Look back over the last chapter and multiply everything by three. There will be tremendous peaks and dips in the response as a result of the modes lining up and interfering with each other. If you have any choice at all, avoid a cubical room for your control room or recording space.

2. The second worst possible dimensions result in a square room with a different ceiling height, for example, a 10-foot by 10-foot room with an 8-foot ceiling. The 10×10 dimension will result in the same modes for two dimensions, increasing the low-frequency problems in the room.

3. An equally bad scenario is when two or three of the dimensions of the room are multiples of each other or of the same number. An example would be 16 feet long by 10 feet wide by 8 feet high. The 16-foot length dimension is divisible by the 8-foot height dimension, so both will have the same modes. Even worse would be an example such as 21 feet long by 14 feet wide by 7 feet high—all three dimensions are multiples of seven and will have the same modes.

4. Some studio designers base the dimensions for their rooms on particular ratios. A common ratio in studio design has long been the "Golden Mean"—the ratio of 0.618, which some feel is ideal for spacing the modes in the room. Dimensions such as 16 feet long by 10 feet wide (a ratio of 16:10) and 24 feet long by 15 feet wide (a ratio of 24:15) come very close to hitting the Golden Mean. If all three dimensions for the room come close to the Golden Mean—for example, 24 feet long by 15 feet wide by 9 feet tall (a ratio of 24:15:9)—the modes of the room will be distributed in a good way.

While the Golden Mean was long considered the ideal, with the availability of computers, other ratios have been found that in some cases result in even better modal distribution, and, as importantly, allow the construction of a room that will work well, but that fits within a given space better. This is a big deal when you're renting a commercial space and you need to construct a studio that fits within it, yet uses the area to its maximum potential.

In general, you're best off to keep your room as large as possible (dirigible hangars may be pushing it a bit), and to hopefully have decent dimensions to work with. Keep this in mind if you're thinking of adding a wall to a larger room in order to have a separate recording space. You may be better off from a dimension standpoint to stay with one larger room that can serve as both recording and control room space.

One of my previous studios was one large room. While working in a one-room studio makes it somewhat difficult to get complete isolation between tracks and you end up having to monitor on headphones when tracking, there are benefits to having the engineer, the producer (if there is one), and the musician(s) in the same room during tracking and overdubbing. And if you have more than one musician, having them perform together in one space at the same time will often result in better performances, especially with musicians who haven't done a lot of studio recording or aren't accustomed to overdubbing. Working in one room tends to reduce the "under the microscope" and "in the spotlight" feeling that many musicians get in a studio with separate recording and control room spaces.

Figure 4.1
The proper combination of length (L), height (H), and width (W) dimensions will result in a pleasing distribution of room modes across the frequency range.

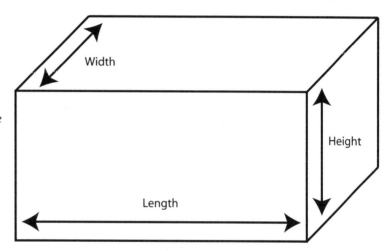

Room Shapes

As you can see from the dimensions discussed earlier, the best room shape is rectangular. (Actually, there are advantages to a non-rectangular room of the right shape, but the construction of such a room is beyond the scope of this book.) Ideally, the rectangular room will have dimensions that either meet or approach some ratio with favorable modal distribution, or at least dimensions that aren't multiples of one another.

Alcoves in one wall of the room, angled walls that cut off part of the rectangular shape, niches, ductwork that descends from the ceiling, "jogs" in walls—all of these can cause resonances and reflection problems. For best results, the room should be as symmetrical as possible when facing forward from the engineer's listening position. In other words, if the room isn't symmetrical, it is best if the asymmetrical areas are behind the listener. Watch out for curves and angles that can reflect sound back to the listening position and cause problems.

It's Not the End of the World

So you've broken out the tape measure and carefully noted the length, width, and height of your room. Don't feel depressed if your room's dimensions are multiples of each other or don't come anywhere close to the Golden Mean ratio, or whatever evaluation criteria are being used.

In the "old days," the BBC decided that a room with 1,500 cubic feet in volume was the minimum size that could be used as a studio for critical listening. (A variety of dimensions will give this room volume, such as 15 feet long by 10 feet wide by 10 feet high, or roughly 15 feet long by 12 feet wide by 8 feet high.) But times have changed, and we have a lot of very effective acoustic materials available to us these days. Even more important, there's a lot more *information* available on how to deal with problem acoustics. A *lot* of us are creating music in rooms that are much smaller than this with fine results, thank you very much. (To be fair, C.L.S. Gilford, who discussed the 1,500-cubic-foot minimum in his article "The Acoustic Design of Talks Studios and Listening Rooms" in *Journal of the*

Audio Engineering Society, January/February 1979 issue, and the BBC had good reason for their room volume specification. But we'll ignore it anyway....)

It just takes some thought and effort. With a bit of acoustic treatment, you can put together a room of almost any dimensions that sounds remarkably accurate and that will yield fine recorded tracks and transportable mixes.

CHAPTER 5

Acoustic Treatments

Now that we've figured out a little bit about what causes acoustical problems in a room, let's take a look at what materials we can use to correct those problems. The good news is that you can easily build and install many types of acoustic treatments yourself with little or no difficulty, not much investment of time, and not much woodworking skill. Of course, to make things look "professional"—or even just good-looking enough to pass the "WAF" (Wife Acceptance Factor—or, more politically correct, "SAF," Spouse Acceptance Factor) or "Pretty Police," as they are sometimes known—will take some knowledge of how to work with tools and materials.

(Note: While I jest about the WAF and Pretty Police, there is good reason to make things look nice: Most musicians perform better in a room that not only sounds good, but also *feels* and *looks* good. The whole "interior design for studios" topic is beyond what we're covering in this book, but keep in mind that the right vibe and look can go a long way toward making a studio a great place in which to be creative.)

What if you're not the handiest person in the world? After all, you're a musician or recording engineer, not a woodworker or furniture craftsman! Fear not, there are numerous companies out there that will be more than happy to provide you with whatever acoustic treatments you might need, at pretty much whatever price point you want to be at.

Why Not Just Use EQ?

Let's get this one out of the way because it always comes up. We're all high-tech to one degree or another—we love playing with our electronic studio toys and gadgets! So why not just get a high-quality graphic or parametric EQ and fix the sound of the room right at the source: the speakers. The answer is: Of course, you can certainly take this approach! I know one Nashville-based studio designer who has a whole system he's devised for equalizing a room into good shape. I've spoken with several of his clients, and they are all quite happy with the results.

There are also monitors available that have parametric equalization capabilities built right into the speaker cabinet—JBL is a big proponent of this with their LSR 6300- and LSR 4300-series monitors. The 4300s are even intelligent enough to automatically figure out what frequency needs to be equalized the most and how much it needs to be cut. Beyond this, many active (powered) monitors have some sort of low- and/or high-frequency filtering (EQ) built in. If you place the monitor close to a wall, you filter the low end to compensate. If the room is overly dull, boost the high frequency filter a bit to make it sound right.

There are a couple of things to be aware of when using EQ in this way. First, EQs can cause phase distortion in a signal, which is never a desirable thing. Most engineers prefer to keep the signal path of their audio as "pure" as possible; while EQ applied to monitors won't be recorded into the tracks or the master mix, you will hear everything through that EQ, and you may make undesired compensations based on any coloration the EQ introduces in the monitors.

Second, modal problems have very narrow bandwidth—as narrow as a single frequency. Few, if any, EQs can conjure up a bandwidth that narrow, so you may be affecting frequencies that don't need to be affected or pushing up or pulling down adjacent frequencies more than they require.

A bigger problem with EQ results from what we saw in Chapter 3: Low-frequency response varies from location to location in the room. Let's say you're equalizing the monitors to sound correct at your listening position. The listening position happens to be a "hot" spot where there's a big peak at a particular frequency. So you go to your EQ and pull that frequency down to balance the sound. Sounds better at the listening position, right? But move your head just a few inches to one side or the other, and you may find yourself located in a dip in the response at that frequency, with that dip now compounded by the EQ you've applied to correct the listening position—a double-whammy.

Finally, recent research is showing that the decay (reverb) time for modes may be as big of a problem as the level variations (the peaks and dips). Equalization does nothing to reduce the decay time at all—EQ is solely about reducing or increasing the level of a particular band of frequencies.

So should you use EQ? Try it if you like…you may find it works for you. But be sure to add up the costs; a good EQ can run quite a few dollars. How many broadband absorbers could you build for that same money?

My recommendation is to get the room sounding as good as you can with acoustic treatment. You may find you don't need any EQ at that point. Or you may want try to tweak things even more to get that last iota of correction once you have the treatments in place, and especially once the reverberant decay of the room is smoothed out across the frequency range.

One tip: If you do decide to use an EQ on your monitors, only use it to cut, not to boost. Boosting could strain your amplifiers and potentially blow your drivers. But more important, boosting has been shown not to provide much compensation for low-frequency cancellations.

But my bet is that once you have your room properly treated, you won't feel the need to invest in an equalizer.

High-Frequency Absorbers

Almost anything soft can provide high-frequency absorption to one degree or another. Still there are some materials that work better than others. Common household materials that provide some mid- and high-frequency control include curtains and drapes, blankets, pillows, clothing, carpet, and so on. And as we'll see in Chapter 10, "No-Budget Home Studio Plan," you can put some of those materials to good use if you have little or no budget to work with. And even if you have treated the room with other materials, you may find that adding some curtains to a window or placing some pillows around can provide some extra absorption around the room.

GLASS FIBER

For creating do-it-yourself absorbers, one of the best and most cost-effective materials you can use is glass fiber, in particular rigid glass fiber. Fluffy glass fiber, like the pink stuff you roll out in attics, has its uses as well, such as for packing into spaces or laying on top of a drop ceiling. But rigid glass fiber is easier to work with and allows for creating panels that can be placed wherever you need absorption. The rigid glass fiber we're talking about comes in thicknesses of up to 5 inches, usually in 2-foot by 4-foot or 4-foot by 8-foot boards. It's available with or without metallic facing on one side; having the facing can be advantageous for some applications. (The facing reduces high-frequency absorption a bit—it reflects high frequencies—which is a good thing if your room is becoming too dead.) The go-to rigid glass fiber for many do-it-yourselfers is the Owens Corning 700-series, specifically types 703 and 705. Another product you can look for is called "ductboard," which may be less expensive.

Ductboard often has black facing on one side to contain the fibers.

The rigid glass fiber boards are fairly easy to work with; you can cut the boards if necessary, and they can be mounted in a variety of ways, including standing them on shelves or simply impaling them on spikes that are stuck in the wall.

Figure 5.1
Because the back of the glass fiber panel will be against the wall, there's no need to wrap it completely.

There are some caveats associated with working with glass fiber, of course. Any fibers that are released from the boards are irritants and can cause itching—and you certainly don't want to inhale them! Wear a long-sleeved shirt and gloves to protect your arms and hands, as well as a mask so you don't breathe any fibers when working with boards. For the sake of anyone in your studio, you'll need to cover the glass fiber with cloth so no one brushes against the raw material. Burlap is a common covering choice, but any cloth you can breathe through is open enough to allow sound to pass through and be absorbed by the glass. (Acoustone is one source for grille cloth that can also be used to cover panels; Guilford of Maine is another source for acoustically "transparent" fabric.) The fabric can be simply cut to shape and glued to the glass fiber. It's not necessary to completely cover the back of the panel with fabric.

If you don't want to deal with covering raw glass fiber, a number of companies sell glass fiber boards that are already covered with fabric, including RPG, Auralex Acoustics, Acoustics First, Acoustical Treatments, and others. (Check out the Appendix for contact information for these and the other companies mentioned in this book.) Some of these, such as those from Auralex, feature hardened edges that are beveled for an attractive appearance.

ACOUSTIC FOAM

If you don't want to do it yourself and you can't afford pre-wrapped glass fiber panels, then acoustic foam is a great option. Foam comes in at a much lower price than pre-covered glass fiber panels and is very easy to deal with. You can simply glue it to your walls, or, if you don't want something that permanent, glue the foam to a light board and hang it from the wall like a picture. I've even hung foam panels using thumbtacks and T-pins. It's fairly easy to cut foam panels into smaller pieces using an electric carving knife; I've also used a pair of heavy shears and a serrated bread knife for this purpose.

Foam is available in different thicknesses—1-inch, 2-inch, 4-inch. Auralex even offers a 12-inch-thick foam panel that works as a bass trap. The thicker the foam, the lower the frequency it will absorb. Usually the foam panels come in 2-foot by 4-foot sheets, although other forms are available. The face of the foam is usually sculpted into pyramids, wedges, or some other shape. This sculpting is for more than just looks. The wedges and pyramids increase the effectiveness of the foam sheet in absorbing tangential and oblique modes; with these types of modes, the sound wave strikes the panel at an angle, and sending it through a wedge or pyramid means that it effectively sees more thickness to pass through.

I've treated several studios using foam panels, and the results can be excellent. Occasionally foam gets a bad rap in Internet discussion forums, but in reality, it's an effective, easy, inexpensive solution to treating a room. In fact, as you'll see in Table 5.1 in the next section of this chapter, 4-inch acoustical foam performs nearly as well as 2-inch rigid glass fiber. Foam solutions are available from Primacoustic, Auralex Acoustics, Illbruck/Sonex, and others.

RATING ACOUSTIC MATERIALS

As you're comparing acoustic materials for treating your studio, it helps to have some kind of basis for making decisions on what works best. One baseline you can use for comparisons is *NRC*—Noise Reduction Coefficient, which shows the overall performance of the material. To determine the NRC for an acoustic material, a test lab measures the response of a reverberant room. Then some of the material is placed in the room and measurements are taken again. A bit of math later—calculating the average of the absorption at 250, 500, 1,000, and 2,000 Hz and rounding off to the nearest 0.05—and the lab has a figure indicating how the acoustic material performs. However, because NRC shows overall performance, rather than performance for a given frequency band, it's not extremely useful for our purposes.

A more useful comparison is using acoustic coefficients, which show the absorptive qualities of an acoustic material for different frequency bands.

In Table 5.1 we see the absorption coefficients for three Auralex Acoustics products at several different octaves, as well as the overall NRC for each product.

Table 5.1 Absorption Coefficients							
	125	**250**	**500**	**1000**	**2000**	**4000**	**NRC**
1" Studiofoam	0.10	0.13	0.30	0.68	0.94	1.00	0.50
4" Studiofoam	0.31	0.85	1.25	1.14	1.06	1.09	1.10
C24 2" glass fiber panel	0.42	0.89	1.12	1.07	1.10	1.09	1.05

Courtesy of Auralex Acoustics, Inc.

As with any test data, the information provided by NRC and absorption coefficients is one more piece of data to help you narrow down your search. Of course, it's not the only thing you should consider by any stretch of the imagination. Combine it with other factors, such as ease of working with the product and mounting it to walls and so on, to make your decision.

BROADBAND ABSORBERS AND BASS TRAPS

As we discussed in the last chapter, there are several different types of bass traps and broadband absorbers. As with high-frequency absorbers, there are commercially available products from a number of companies. These range from foam and glass fiber absorbers, to wooden panel traps, to membrane resonators.

DIY

There are several ways to easily make your own bass traps. The simplest solution? Buy a bale of fluffy glass fiber or three, and stack them in the corners of your room. (While this will work fine, it doesn't have very high aesthetic value and it takes up quite a bit of space.)

For many home and project studios, a good-looking, inexpensive, and easy solution is our new friend, the rigid glass fiber panel. Panels wrapped in fabric and placed across the corners of the room make for very effective broadband absorbers. Wall-to-wall corners are prime for this type of treatment, but you can also place panels across wall-to-ceiling corners and even floor-to-wall corners, though you have to be careful with these that clients and studio visitors don't step on them. For the greatest possible absorption, place the panels across the wall-to-wall-to-ceiling junctions. The panels can be mounted by impaling them on spikes in the wall or by building shelves in the corner on which to stack the panels.

Figure 5.2
Rigid glass fiber panels mounted across a wall-to-wall corner make effective broadband absorbers.

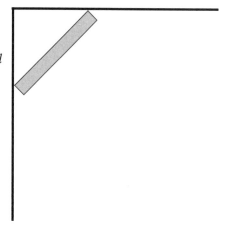

Another solution using glass fiber: Cut each 2-foot by 4-foot glass fiber board into four triangles, then stack the resulting glass fiber pieces on top of each other in the corners from floor to ceiling, and cover the front of the stack with fabric. The result is a corner filled with absorptive material and effective bass trapping.

Figure 5.3
Cutting a 4-foot by 2-foot glass fiber board into four large triangles.

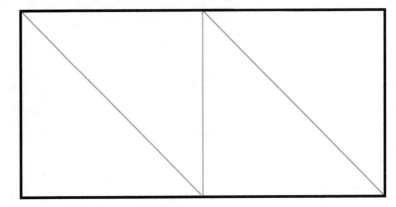

Figure 5.4
A glass fiber board can also be cut into eight smaller triangles.

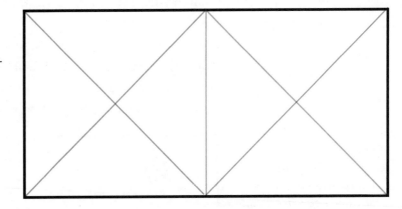

Figure 5.5
Stacking glass fiber triangles
from floor to ceiling in a cor-
ner creates a good bass trap.
The front of the stack should
be covered with fabric to pre-
vent glass fiber strands from
getting into the room.

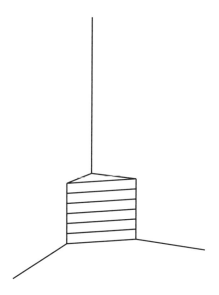

COMMERCIAL

With commercial bass traps and broadband absorbers, there are a number of solutions. Companies such as RPG and StudioPanels manufacture tuned resonator traps. RealTraps makes several varieties of bass trap panels that are designed to be placed across corners, similar to how we discussed using glass fiber panels earlier.

Several companies, including Primacoustic and Auralex Acoustics, make affordable foam bass traps that can be placed in room corners; Auralex, in particular, makes a variety of foam bass traps that function over a wide frequency range. Foam traps function as broadband absorbers and, because they are foam, also help control reverberant decay and high frequencies in the room. Auralex also makes glass fiber panels that are pre-wrapped and mitered on the edges to mount cleanly into corners. ASC (*Acoustic Sciences Corporation*) makes tube traps that can be placed in corners to serve as bass traps as well.

The advantage to manufactured bass traps is the convenience and ease of use. Just mount them (or even stand them) in the corners, and you're good to go.

Diffusion

Building your own diffusors is a difficult proposition. It's easy to mount or stack items against the walls in a room to create some degree of redirection of the sound waves. But true diffusion—scientifically scattering the sound waves based on mathematical calculations—is difficult to achieve.

Figure 5.6
A regular bookcase loaded with books can make a useful "pseudo-diffusor" for placement in a studio. While the result won't be true diffusion, sound waves will be broken up by the various books and surfaces.

DIY solutions for redirecting sound include mounting curved or angled wooden panels on walls or placing items with irregular depth against a wall, somewhat mimicking a quadratic diffusor. (See the section later in this chapter called, "Quadratic Diffusors.") One common way to do this is to position a bookcase against the wall at the point where you want diffusion, then fill its shelves with books of varying depths. You won't get "true" diffusion, but you will break up sound wave reflections and redirect the waves in various ways. I've used this approach in studios, and it does provide a workable and—if you already own (and hopefully have read) the books—an affordable solution.

COMMERCIAL SOLUTIONS

It's probably no surprise that several companies manufacture diffusors that can be installed in your studio. Auralex Acoustics makes some of the more affordable diffusors, molded into various shapes from lightweight plastic. Several of these products will drop right into a standard 2-foot by 2-foot drop-ceiling grid. Primacoustic also makes the "Polyfuser," which combines a varying elliptical-shape for dispersing sound waves with bass-trap functionality.

QUADRATIC DIFFUSORS

RPG was one of the first manufacturers of quadratic residue diffusors, which use mathematical formulas for generating a random pattern on the surface of a diffusor. The idea is to arrange wells, or blocks or strips of wood or other materials, into an array, each at a different depth. The varying surface breaks up sound as the waves are reflected from the panel. The more wells, blocks, or strips there are for a given area, the better the high-frequency diffusion; the deeper the wells or variations in blocks or strips, the better the low-frequency performance.

Auralex recently introduced the SpaceArray, which provides the same function, and Primacoustic makes their Razorblade panels. All of these products are easy to use;

simply mount them to the walls or ceiling of your studio in appropriate places, and you're finished.

Figure 5.7
Quadratic diffusors use an array of different height or depth surfaces to break up and disperse sound waves.

Making your own quadratic residue diffusors is something of a challenge. There are plans available on the Internet for building your own, but you'll need woodworking skills. For most small rooms (which includes almost all home and project studios), absorption is a much easier solution for taming acoustics than trying to make your own diffusion.

Studio Treatment in a Box

Several companies, including Primacoustic, Auralex Acoustics, and StudioPanel, have stepped up to the plate with "kits" for acoustically treating rooms. These kits make it easy. Various configurations are provided for dealing with different-sized rooms. The kits include absorption, bass traps, and, depending on the room size the kit is intended for, some diffusion as well. If you're looking for an easy solution, kits can be a workable one: Order the one you want, install it according to the instructions, and start making music. If you find you want more absorption or bass trapping, you can always add to the contents of the kit.

CHAPTER 6

Acoustic Myths

As with any field that combines art and science, there are a lot of acoustical myths and misconceptions that have flourished over the years. And as with all such myths, these and others die a hard death. Let's look at the facts behind a few fallacies that have hung on for far too long.

Egg Cartons

This is a stubborn one. Someone somewhere got the idea that sticking empty egg cartons on the walls of a room would help with acoustic problems and even provide soundproofing. There's very little truth to it. The material most egg cartons are made from offers a little high-frequency absorption, but it's far too thin and lightweight to provide any kind of mass for sound isolation purposes. About the only thing egg cartons can provide is a somewhat irregular surface for a bit of very high-frequency diffusion. The worst thing about egg cartons is that they're often made from very flammable materials—not safe for a home or business.

Figure 6.1
Rare, indeed! The amazing thing is that people were actually bidding on it. (Names removed to protect the guilty....)

Eat the eggs prepared in your favorite fashion and toss or recycle the cartons.

Holy Eggs

Renowned studio designer Russ Berger tells this story:

"We once worked with the director of a Hawaiian public radio station who recounted a story about their first studio. On an excruciatingly tight budget, the original studios were treated with egg cartons. As is their custom with new construction, the local Kahuna was invited out to bless the facility for a small honorarium.

"The Kahuna was a rather large, rotund lady in full native dress, with all the usual acoustical testing accoutrements:

beads, rattles, the works. Upon stepping into the studio for the first time, she grasped her chest in mock horror and circular swoon, and solemnly exclaimed, 'Ohhh, the tortured souls of the dead chickens! This will be very expensive for me to bless and make this right!'

"Over the years I've come to fondly remember her as the ultimate consultant…."

Carpet on the Walls

As with all myths there's a hint of truth hidden in the one about carpet on the walls helping with sound isolation and for controlling reverberation and echo. Soft carpet will provide high-frequency absorption, and if there's a thick pad behind it, may even provide somewhat lower absorption.

Figure 6.2:
The absorptive capabilities of most carpet drops off very quickly in the mid frequencies and is non-existent at low frequencies. (Courtesy of Auralex Acoustics, Inc.)

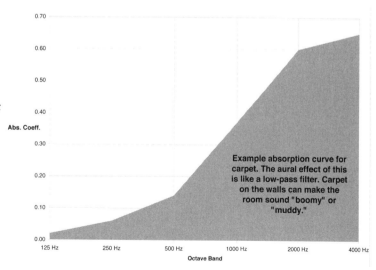

Example absorption curve for carpet. The aural effect of this is like a low-pass filter. Carpet on the walls can make the room sound "boomy" or "muddy."

But most carpet is too thin to work very low in the frequency range. Of course, there are many varieties of carpet. But in general, there isn't enough mass with any type to provide any semblance of sound isolation. And there's a bigger potential problem. Because carpet doesn't absorb very low, the reverberant decay balance tends to be thrown off, leaving the low end resonating in the room. As with all such "treatments," you'll need bass trapping (and probably some sort of midrange absorption) to balance things out.

I've been in too many band rehearsal rooms where the musicians have lined the walls with carpet (in some cases, salvaged from places better left unexplored). The result is a dark, muffled-sounding room with boomy low end.

Carpet on the floor isn't the end of the world acoustically—in fact, I like having a nice, warm, soft carpet underfoot when working. But on the walls or the ceiling… generally not a good idea acoustically.

Any Foam Will Work

In an effort to save a few dollars, many musicians and home studio owners have tried to get by with non-acoustic foam, substituting foam mattresses, dense packing foam, pillow foam, whatever. It's true that almost any soft material will absorb sound waves to one extent or another, but these materials simply can't compare to the performance of acoustic foam. True acoustic foam has its shape optimized for acoustical performance and appearance; foam like that used in bedding is optimized for comfort and support. Most important, true acoustic foam is an "open cell" material that allows the sound energy to easily pass through, where it is converted to heat. Other types of foam don't do the job anywhere near as well.

Furniture Solves Acoustic Problems

There is some truth to this one; we've already talked about using a bookcase to provide a sort of diffusion. Likewise, a well-placed sofa, couch, or overstuffed chair can indeed provide some bass trapping. And if it's covered with a soft material (not leather or vinyl), it will also provide some absorption at higher frequencies. As nice as that may sound, you can't count on acoustic performance that equals a real bass trap or broadband absorber. Still, you need to sit, right? And if you can sit on a piece of furniture that may help the sound of the room, why not?

In fact, Jeff Szymanski, former Chief Acoustical Engineer at Auralex Acoustics, did some analysis of a room empty, and after adding two couches. According to his report, entitled "Effects of Couches on Low-Frequency Response," originally posted on Recording.org, "[T]he effect on the low-frequency response was not huge. However, some smoothing and some general reduction in level [was] present." Szymanski noted that the couch did provide much better performance at reducing the reverberant decay time in the low-frequency range. "It is particularly interesting to note the significant decrease in modal decay across the low-frequency range after the couches [were] added. This decrease was quite audible, most notably in the range above 100 Hz."

As for other furniture, the effect it will have on the acoustics in a studio is likely minimal. And in reality, furniture with large flat surfaces may in fact cause problematic reflections. That isn't to say you shouldn't have furniture in your room. But be careful where you place it so you minimize any potential problems.

Bass Trapping Takes a Lot of Space

This one probably developed as musicians visited large commercial facilities and noted the size and depth of the bass traps that were built into the rooms. There's just no way that there's room in most home or project studios for that sort of treatment.

And there is some truth to this statement. If you want to absorb very low frequencies with foam, you are going to need a thick mass—at 30 Hz, we're talking a porous absorber at least four feet deep! Even a wooden panel trap would have to be at least 10 to 11 inches deep to reach that low in frequency. In general, you can say that where bass treatment is concerned, bigger is better for the best possible results.

Fortunately, you can achieve good performance with smaller treatments. Research has shown that there are ways to absorb low end without using massive pieces of material. Plus, we've learned some techniques, such as treating the corners of the room, that don't take up so much floor space. And manufacturers have stepped up with more compact bass traps that will work in smaller rooms.

EQ Can Solve All Acoustic Problems

We discussed this back in Chapter 4. EQ can reduce the level of modal peaks in a room. However, it does nothing to counter the spatial dependence of modes (where moving your head puts you into a different modal peak or null than at the listening position) and it has no effect on the time dependence of the mode, either. (EQ can't reduce decay or reverb time in a room.)

Opinions vary on the effectiveness of EQ for treating rooms. It definitely gives some engineers and musicians what they want. My opinion (not to repeat what I already said a few pages ago): Treat the room acoustically first. Then, if you desire, apply EQ to tweak things even more.

Part II

Treating Your Studio

CHAPTER 7

Choosing the Best Room for Your Studio

Many home and project studio owners don't have a great deal of choice about where their studios will be located. It comes down to where there's space, where things are out of the way, or what room isn't being used for another purpose by the rest of the family. Still, when thinking about where your studio is going to end up living, there are some things to keep in mind. We discussed room dimensions and shapes in Chapter 4. If possible, those two considerations should be your primary concern. But there are other things to think about.

Isolationism

It's a *very* rare studio that doesn't make some noise now and then. Maybe if you only do instrumental music and all your sounds come from synths and samplers, you can get by monitoring only on headphones.

But that's not ideal. And most studios are eventually going to have the need to put a microphone on something—vocals, guitars, or some other sound source. In order to do it well, you'll need isolation. If you're located in a house populated by other humans, there are two concerns—isolation from noise bleeding in from outside your studio and isolation for the rest of the house from the noise you'll be making.

Take a look at the rooms that are available to you, and choose the one that's farthest from the rest of the house (see the inverse square law in Chapter 13, "Sound Isolation"), and is the most off the beaten path. This may be the bedroom that is farthest from the main family areas, it may be in the basement, or it may mean making the attic or garage into a livable space where you can record without being disturbed and without disturbing others.

There's not much you can do short of major construction to keep a screaming Marshall stack (or even a wound up AC30) from rocking the house, and it's nearly impossible to isolate a drum set. But for reasonable-volume sounds and monitor levels, choosing the most isolated room will help at least a little bit in maintaining the family peace.

Bedrooms

A pretty high percentage of home and project studios end up in spare bedrooms. Not a bad place to be, in a lot of ways. Unfortunately, most spare bedrooms aren't optimized for acoustic response. They often are nearly square in shape, plus they have inconveniently (from an acoustic standpoint) located doors, closets, and windows. But with some acoustic treatment, you can make things work very well. And the closets come in very handy as isolation booths for noisy computers, for recording guitar amps, or even for vocalists, if the closet is large enough.

Attics

If your house has an attic that's habitable or can be made habitable, this might be a good space for locating your studio. Finding enough ceiling height may be an issue, but depending on how things are set up, it could be a possibility. Just be conscious of where you're located in relation to the house below you—avoid placing the studio over a bedroom where someone will be trying to sleep at the same time you are trying to make recordings.

Basements

Basements offer one big advantage: Being at least partially underground, they offer good isolation from surrounding residences, which will help preserve your relations with the neighbors if things get loud. However, you won't be very isolated from the house above you, so, as with attics, be conscious of where you place the studio in relation to the rooms overhead. If you choose an unfinished basement location, be sure that it is dry and clean.

Unless you have a "walkout" or "daylight" basement, you probably won't have to contend with too many windows, which is a plus. However, you may be faced with mechanical noise from furnaces, cooling systems, and fans.

Garages

If you're getting serious about your studio and you want to take it up a few notches, one solution is to remodel your garage into a studio space. You'll give up your parking and storage, but you may gain an ideal room in which to work. It's going to take some effort. For best results, you'll need to build a room within the garage, with its own heating, cooling, and ventilation, and power lines. The advantage is that the resulting room-within-a-room construction can provide great isolation from the rest of the world.

Finding a Corner

Can't find a room in which to place your studio? Live in a small apartment with no spare room? It doesn't mean you can't have a studio! I've used the kitchen table, a corner of the living room, part of the home office, wherever I could find some space to set up my equipment. It's difficult to do much acoustic treatment with this kind of a setup, but one option is to make some movable panels that you can set up to absorb around your monitors or sources that you're trying to record.

The important thing is to find somewhere you can work on your music! Once you've got a place, you can get down to the business of treating that location for the best possible acoustics you can achieve.

CHAPTER 8

Getting Started

So you've decided on the room your studio is going to live in, and you're ready to start treating it for better sound. Congratulations! You're close to making music in your new space.

Before you get too far into things, it can be really useful to take a look at your space, to get a feel for what you have to work with acoustically. We'll be doing a "real" analysis of the room later in this chapter, so the following tests aren't required. But I've found it to be interesting and revealing to have some ears-on comparisons of the "before" and "after" room.

Start with an empty room. For one thing, it's a lot easier to install acoustic treatments before you have all your gear and furniture loaded in and arranged. Differences are also more apparent when you compare the "raw" empty room to the final treated studio with everything installed and set up.

Bring in your monitors and amplifier/mixer (if you don't have powered monitors), and something to play test tones, sweeps, and music so you can hear the raw room. If you need a source for test tones, there are a number of "studio tools" CDs available commercially that feature them. You can download a CD's-worth of tones for free from the RealTraps Web site (http://www.realtraps.com). Auralex Acoustics has tone sweeps that are available for free download on their site (http://www.auralex.com). Plug-in manufacturer Audio Ease (http://www.audioease. com) makes a $29.95 program for the Mac called "Make A TestTone" that generates tones and sweeps as audio files on your computer.

Figure 8.1
Audio Ease's Make A TestTone for the Mac generates tones and sweeps, among other things.

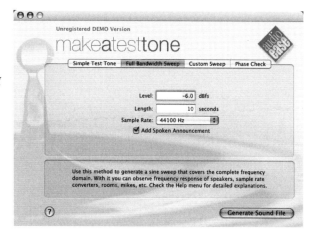

You can either burn any of these tones and sweeps to an audio CD for playback on a CD player, or play them from your computer or other audio player. I prefer to use a CD player because it doesn't add much to the background noise; computers can be noisy. (We'll talk about how to control computer noise in Chapter 12, "Noise Control.")

A useful tool for learning about your room (and for your studio to have around) is a sound level meter. You can go all out and purchase a very expensive one with lots of bells and whistles, or you can do what I did: Go to Radio Shack. The Shack stocks two models; one uses an analog "needle"-type meter (catalog #33-4050), and the other has a digital display (catalog #33-2055). I sprang for the extra few bucks for the digital one, but either will work fine, and at a price that won't hit the bank account too hard.

The first thing that I do when I walk into a room is to sharply clap my hands a few times in various places in the space. The idea is to listen for flutter echo problems, to hear whether there is high-frequency ringing in the room, and to get a feel for whether the room has a "boxy" sound quality. Don't despair if your room exhibits these qualities; if you're in an empty rectangular space with hard walls, it's pretty much guaranteed that you will hear some amount of flutter echo and ringing. That's just the nature of the beast! Make note of what you're hearing so you can come back in after treating the room and hear the difference.

Doing the Walk-Around

Set up your test rig in the room—if you have an idea of how you want the studio set up, go ahead and put the monitor speakers where you think they might end up, on some sort of stands that will place them near ear-level height when you're seated.

If you have no clue how you want your studio arranged, never fear; we'll be covering that in detail in the next chapter. We're not doing anything final right now; this is just for test purposes—to excite the modes in the room so we can hear what's happening in it.

For now, try placing the monitors so that they "fire" the long way in the room, 2 to 3 feet away from the wall behind them, and symmetrically placed side-to-side in the room.

Play long, sustained low-frequency tones through one monitor (mute, disconnect, or turn off the other). Break out your meter and adjust the speaker volume so the C-weighted levels average around 80 to 85 dB for the various tones. Walk around the room, stopping to listen in various places. You'll likely hear that at some places, a given tone will be louder, and at other places, it will be lower in volume. Some tones will also likely be much louder than other tones—room modes at work! Once again, make note of what you're hearing in various places—it doesn't hurt to jot down a few impressions on a notepad—so you can compare the results after the room is treated.

Sweeping Up

Here's another preliminary test you can do to start getting a feel for your room. You'll be using one monitor speaker as mentioned in the previous section. Place the sound level meter at the spot you're figuring will be the engineer's listening position. Now play a frequency sweep through the monitor (you really only need to go through the low frequencies), and watch what happens on the meter. As the tone sweeps through the various frequencies, you'll likely see the level on the meter fluctuating pretty drastically. Yes, that's the effects of room modes and cancellations you're seeing. It's hard to make any kind of quantitative judgments about what you're seeing because at this point, you can't tell exactly which frequencies are louder and which are softer. But try to get a feel for how large the swings are from loud peaks to soft dips so you can compare after the studio is finished. (Remember to take into account the spatial effects of modes; what you see on the meter may not line up with what you're hearing from where you're listening.)

At this point, I like to play a variety of music with both speakers on to get a feel for what the room sounds like with full-bandwidth musical material playing in it. Choose material that you know very well and have heard in a variety of locations. I have created a custom "compilation" CD with reference music on it that I use for familiarizing myself with different rooms and monitor speakers. It features a range of musical and production styles—over the years I've honed in on a list of songs and instrumental pieces that each tells me something about the space and the speakers.

Notice what you're hearing. Listen closely to different frequency ranges. Is the bass boomy? Muddy? The highs shrill? Are the mids harsh or edgy? Is the room mushy or overly echo-y? When you stop the player, does the sound keep ringing or echoing in the room? It's a good bet your room exhibits some or all of these problems. Listen closely; can you hear *into* the mix? Unless you're inordinately lucky or are listening to an enchanted room, probably not. However, keep the sound you're hearing in your memory so you can compare after treating the room.

Analyzing Your Room

To really understand what is happening in your room, true analysis is required. There are two big reasons for analyzing your room:

1. By analyzing the empty room, you gain valuable information that you can use to help decide what sorts of acoustic treatment you should use—you'll be able to see the various modes, and will also (with the right sort of analysis) get an idea of the room's reverberant decay and RT60 characteristics.

2. By analyzing the empty room, you'll have a benchmark or starting place; then, if you analyze again after treating the room, you'll be able to see how much difference the treatment made in the sound of the room. And you'll know whether there are any remaining acoustical anomalies that need to be fixed or that you should be aware of.

There are a couple of different ways to do in-depth analysis of your room. A good solution is to purchase a piece of software that will provide data on the room's response. There are several reasonably priced packages that can do a good job of figuring out what your room is doing. Two Windows/PC programs that are commonly used are ETF by AcoustiSoft and Smaart Acoustic Tools by SIA Software Company. (Check in the Appendix at the end of the book for contact information for these and other companies mentioned throughout this book.) Unfortunately, I haven't found a program I like as well for the Macintosh, though some users report having luck running ETF in a Windows emulator on the Mac, and others like SpectraFoo from Metric Halo Labs. There are also hardware analyzers available, such as the Terrasonde Audio Toolbox and the NTI (NT Instruments) AL1 Acoustilyzer.

Most forms of analysis operate in much the same way. You play a frequency sweep in the room and record the results with a microphone placed at the listening (or other) position in the room. The resulting recording is loaded into the analysis program, which spits out a variety of graphs and information describing the acoustic response in the room, RT60 or reverberant decay, and much more (in fact, much more information than most of us need).

DIY Analysis

For a rough idea of what is happening in your room, you can try the "do-it-yourself" approach to analysis. If you'd like to try it, as mentioned earlier, RealTraps has download-able test tone audio files and printable audio (logarithmic) graph paper on their site. The idea is that you play each tone, measuring its level with your handy Radio Shack level meter. (Be sure to set the meter for "C" weighting and "slow" response, and note that the response below 50 Hz may not be completely accurate….) Print out the paper, get busy with a pencil graphing the results, and bingo, you're done.

If you take this approach, be sure that you are using tones that are 1 Hz apart; using 1/3-octave or even 1/6-octave intervals is too wide to accurately show all the peaks and dips in the room's response.

The results won't be quite as accurate as using sweep and analysis software, but you can get a good idea of what's happening, and it's certainly an inexpensive solution. Two big drawbacks: One is that playing and measuring every frequency up to 300 Hz or so takes a fair amount of time. The second is that you don't get any information on the reverberant decay or RT60 in the room, or how balanced the room's decay is. The information you receive from working with just test tones is solely in the level domain.

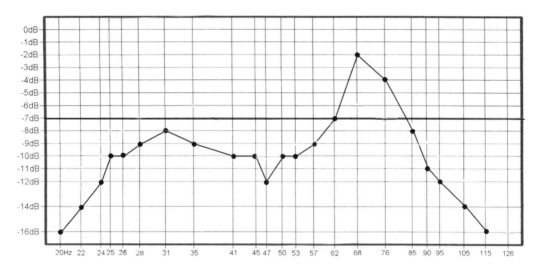

Figure 8.2: Analyzing the frequency response for a room with intervals that are too wide will result in a curve that could miss narrow-bandwidth problems in the response.

Let Someone Else Do It

There's another option for analyzing your room that's tough to beat. Companies such as Auralex Acoustics will analyze sweeps from your room so you can get the full before/after picture. They'll even offer suggestions for what treatments might work best in your room and how to place them. Various levels of service are offered. Some are free, and others involve a fee.

CHAPTER 9

Studio Layout and Treatment

It's time to get started making your studio into the best acoustic environment it can be! First we're going to take a look at how to set your studio up in your room for the best acoustic response. Then we'll look at where treatments should be placed in the room so that they'll work to their fullest capacity.

Getting Oriented

So how should you set up the room? The answer, of course, depends on the room—there are a lot of variables. If you had a rectangular room with great dimensions and no windows or doors, setup would be fairly easy. But few of us have the ideal room, and not having any doors might make working in the room somewhat *challenging*.

Still there are some basic rules of thumb that we can apply to the rooms we do have, making allowances for where our specific rooms don't quite permit the ideal.

First up, let's figure out how the room should be oriented, how the studio should be facing. In general, given a rectangular room, you're acoustically best off having the speakers firing the long way—along the longest dimension in the room. This reduces the effects of reflections returning to the listening position after reflecting from the rear wall.

Figure 9.1
Setting the monitors up so they fire the long way in the room is often a good starting place.

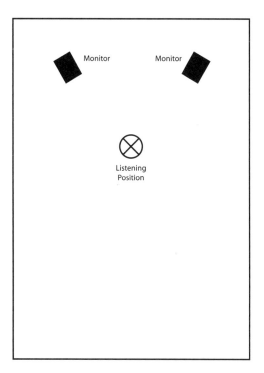

Speaker Placement and Listening Position

The ideal monitor speaker placement is pretty well defined. The standard is to arrange the left and the right speakers so that they form an equilateral triangle with your head. This allows for good "imaging," panning, and placement in the mix. Aiming the speakers so that they are focused slightly behind your head will make the "sweet spot" a bit larger.

Figure 9.2
Set the monitors up so they form an equal-sided triangle with the listening position, aimed at a point slightly behind the listener.

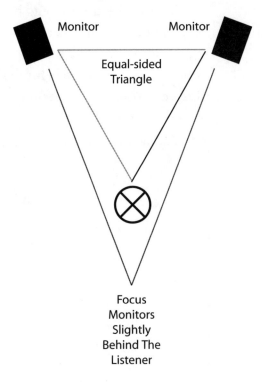

Monitor   Monitor

Equal-sided
Triangle

Focus
Monitors
Slightly
Behind The
Listener

For most accurate response, place the two monitors at least two or three feet from the front wall. Closer to the wall, and you'll get low-end boost. (Some monitors have built-in filters that allow you to compensate for this problem.) The farther the monitors are from the side walls of the room the better, because it will cut down on reflection problems. Of course, we'll be treating those first reflection points later in this chapter, so don't worry too much about this.

One thing you don't want to do is to place the monitors in the corners of the room. Doing so results in a *huge* low-end boost, more than even most built-in filters can correct. Even worse would be to have one monitor in a corner and another not in a corner—the response of the two speakers will be radically different, and it will be very difficult to get a solid stereo mix.

Some studio designers recommend placing the listening position according to the same "Golden Mean" ratio as they recommend for finding the ideal room dimensions. This means that the listening position should be 38% of the way back in the room.

Another "rule" states that the speakers should be placed at a distance equal to 70% of the width of the room from the front wall. This works well as long as the room is longer than it is wide. If you have a room that's 20 feet long by 12 feet wide, the speakers should 0.7×12, or 8.4 feet from the front wall. As the length and width dimensions become closer and closer to equal, this rule works less and less well.

There are other formulas and rules as well; some even help to calculate the optimum distance from the front wall, the side walls, and off the floor. If you don't feel like calculating the positions, you could use a program such as RPG's Room Optimizer, which will place the speakers at a location that minimizes modal and boundary interference effects.

The idea behind using these "rules" and techniques is to find a position that minimizes the effects of any modes in the room. In practice it works well— -although keep in mind that it is important to maintain an equilateral triangle (all sides the same length) with the monitors. To ensure this, place the listening position first, then orient the monitors in an equilateral triangle based on where the listener will be. One thing to keep in mind, no matter how you're figuring out where to place your speakers: Make sure that no two distances are the same; in other words, the distance from the front wall shouldn't equal the distance from the side wall, and so on.

Symmetry

As you are placing your monitors and other equipment in the room, a prime concern should be symmetry. Make sure the left monitor is as far from the left wall as the right monitor is from the right wall. Going back to how you orient your studio, it's also ideal if the room itself is symmetrical. It's hard to create a stable stereo image if one side of the room is different from the other. For example, a wall on one side, but a floor-to-ceiling bookcase on the other isn't as good as two solid walls opposite each other. Likewise, having a wall on one side and a window on the other destroys symmetry.

If the room is asymmetrical, or you're forced for some reason to orient the studio in an asymmetrical fashion, it's best to place the asymmetrical parts behind the listening position. In an L-shaped room, for example, it's best to place the open short side of the L behind the listening position.

Figure 9.3
In an L-shaped room, set up the studio so the short side is behind the listener.

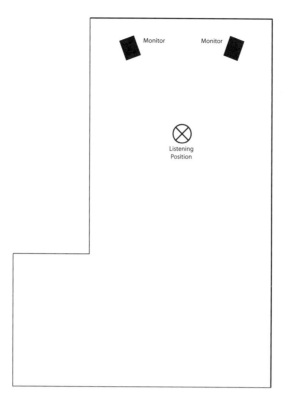

Likewise, it's better if windows and doors are on the side walls behind the mix position. A window between the monitors isn't too bad, but one behind may cause some serious reflections.

The Ultimate Answer

Ultimately, though, you have to place the gear and listening position where it works—meaning where it fits in the room and where you have the fewest compromises. And also where it feels best to sit and work—this may be where you have a window close at hand so you can be inspired by beautiful scenery.

In my current studio, for example (described in Chapter 16, "Studio Gallery: Bedroom"), I seemingly violated a number of rules. The speakers don't fire lengthwise. It's an L-shaped room, and in fact, I'm not even at one end of the room. But for a variety of reasons, including the multipurpose use of the room, the availability of a nearby closet for placing noisy equipment, and most of all, the presence of two great windows for checking out the view outside while I work, the studio ended up where it is. The good news? With some acoustic treatment, this is the best-sounding control room area I've ever had. And it's very comfortable to work there—a big plus in my mind.

Figure 9.4
A rough layout of the author's studio.

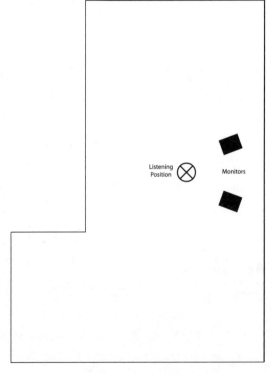

Even studio designers don't always agree on where the best placement and orientation is in a given room. (More on this in Chapter 17, "Visual Representations of Studio

Gallery: Bonus Room.") So observe the rules and try roughly placing the studio in accordance with them—set up just the monitors and whatever you need to play some music for now. Get an idea of how things sound. Then throw the rules out the window and try placing the monitors and playback system where it feels right to place them. Worst case, you have to move the speakers to a few different spots. Try a few different locations and orientations. What works well for you?

Once you've decided what's most comfortable, what feels best, take a look at the area where your gear is set up. How hard is it going to be to hang treatments on the wall and ceiling? What's behind you? Where are the windows and doors? Can you make it all work? In some cases you can, and in some cases you can't. There are always compromises unless you are designing from the ground up. And even then, you still have to allow for doors, storage, equipment, and so on.

Treatment Placement

Finding the right locations in your room to place acoustic treatment materials isn't a difficult task. For a while, the fashion was to make the entire front of the room, around the monitors and listening position, absorptive, while leaving the back of the room live or reflective (the so-called "Live-End/Dead-End" or LEDE™ design). And this type of design can indeed work very well if implemented properly; I've worked in this sort of studio and enjoyed it very much. But these days alternative approaches are accepted, and not everyone likes working in a room with a completely dead front end or a completely live back section—myself included.

GUIDELINES

Here are some guidelines for treatment placement:

1. Bass traps and broadband absorbers work well in the corners, whether wall-to-wall corners, wall-to-ceiling corners, or, rarely (because it can be inconvenient), wall-to-floor corners. Another good spot is the junction of two walls and the ceiling. You don't have to cover from floor to ceiling in the corners, though the more area you cover, the more absorption and trapping you will get. It's also not necessary for the traps to be sealed airtight against the walls. Simply hang or stand them in the corners and they'll work fine.

2. First reflection points should be treated with absorption. But how to find the first reflection points? You could figure it out using high school geometry—you took that class for a reason, right?

   Didn't get a passing geometry grade, or don't feel like breaking out the old protractor? Here's an easy method to find reflection points: Place your monitors where they will be located in the room. Now sit down in the listening position, as if you were working on a mix. Have an accomplice hold a mirror against the wall on one side, roughly centered between your listening position and the speakers. Have your assistant move the mirror until you can see the nearest monitor's high-frequency driver (tweeter) reflected in the glass. This location is the center point of the area that should be treated with absorption—in general a 4-foot square of treatment will do the trick. Repeat for the opposite side of the studio.

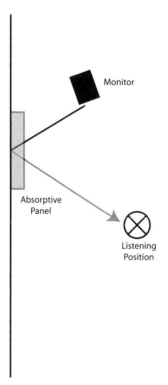

Figure 9.5
A 4-foot square of absorption should be placed at the first reflection point on the side wall between the listener and monitor.

3. You'll also want treatment on the wall behind you. If you're going to use some diffusion, this is a good spot for it. Otherwise, absorption works well, especially for rooms where the distance to the back wall is small. You can certainly use diffusion where the distance to the back wall is short; it will work. It just won't be as effective as it would be with a longer distance.

4. Place absorption on the front wall behind the monitors. It's true that monitors disperse most of their mid and high frequencies from their front side. But treating the wall behind the monitors seems to improve imaging

and helps with any reflections from the back wall or between the monitors and the wall.

Improving Performance

Acoustic foam and glass fiber panels make great absorbers. But they aren't effective very far down into the low frequencies. (Unless the foam is very thick…and who has room for 4-foot-thick panels in their bedroom studio?) Want to get even better low-frequency performance out of your absorptive treatments? Here's an easy way to do it: Mount the panels with an air gap behind them. An inch or two makes a big difference; a larger gap will result in even lower frequency absorption.

You can use spacers behind the panels to create an air gap. For acoustic foam (which isn't rigid and doesn't hang well away from a wall or other surface), one solution I've used in several studios is to glue the foam to lightweight plastic garden lattice. Mount the lattice against spacers to create an air gap behind the foam. (See Chapter 17.)

5. Don't forget the ceiling. Interior designers tell you to treat the ceiling as a fifth wall when you are painting or coming up with a wall treatment. Many designers will tell you the same thing with acoustic treatment and the ceiling: Treat it as a fifth wall.

   If your ceiling is low (7 to 8 feet or less), use absorption at the first reflection points on the ceiling to make it seem higher. If you have a higher ceiling, diffusion can work well on the ceiling for smoothing out the reverberant decay in the room.

You have two installation options with the ceiling. You can mount the treatment right on the ceiling (for example, glue acoustic foam or mount glass fiber panels right on the surface of the ceiling). If you have the height, another solution is to hang a "cloud" over the mix position. The idea is to suspend absorbent panels a foot or more below the ceiling. Doing this creates space above the panels, which allows them to operate down to lower frequencies than they can when placed against a surface. It also allows you to place more absorbent acoustic material on top of the cloud, increasing absorption. The result is that the cloud becomes a broadband absorber, working on frequencies down into the bass range.

Figure 9.6
A ceiling "cloud" is created by suspending absorption or diffusion above the listening position. For better low frequency performance, roll out fluffy glass fiber on top of the cloud.

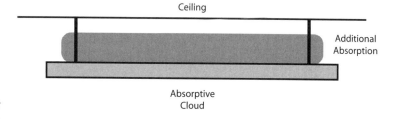

If you have a drop ceiling, you can accomplish much the same thing. Stuff the area between the rafters above the drop ceiling with fluffy glass fiber and roll out fluffy glass fiber on top of the ceiling tiles. You can even replace the ceiling tiles with rigid glass fiber panels cut to fit in the ceiling grid (covered with fabric, of course), then roll out fluffy stuff on top. In this case, you get two benefits: The absorption makes the ceiling seem higher, and the extra absorption depth lets the ceiling function as a broadband absorber/bass trap.

6. It's pretty tough to get much absorptive or diffusive benefit from the floor—in fact, our brains seem wired to be able to ignore the acoustic effects of the floor in critical listening. What's on the floor is more a matter of preference. A carpet on the floor will absorb some high frequencies (and will be cozy underfoot). But, remember our discussion of the myth of carpet on the walls: Absorbing only high frequencies with carpet without absorbing enough lows and mids can unbalance the decay in the room.

Many engineers prefer to work on a wood floor, especially for recording rooms and isolation booths. They like the sound of reflections from the wood for acoustic recordings, and the floor brings back a nice "natural" ambience to a room that's treated with absorption. I've been in studios with concrete floors (painted or stained) that also worked well. I've also seen studios where there was wood under the mix position and carpet around the outside portion of the floor.

If you are going to go with a reflective floor, be sure you have plenty of absorption or diffusion on the ceiling to prevent flutter echo, resonances, or modes from developing.

Creating a Reflection-Free Zone

The concept behind the various treatment placements described earlier is to create a "Reflection-Free Zone" (RFZ™) at the main listening position. Current acoustical thinking isn't to kill the room with absorption; it's to control reflections, tame modes, reduce RT60, and balance reverberant decay times across the frequency range.

By creating an RFZ, you've gone a long way toward controlling reflections. You've also, in conjunction with other absorption in the room, reduced RT60 and, with broadband absorption, balanced the decay time. A little (or a lot) of bass trapping, and you should have a good-sounding room.

The End Result

So when you combine all the treatments, what do you end up with for a basic plan for treating the room? Figure 9.7 shows the way in which all the treatments come together. Naturally you're going to have to adapt to the specifics of your room, but the principles remain the same.

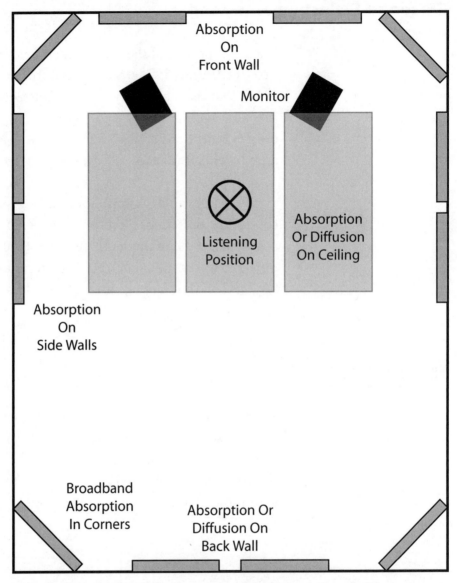

Figure 9.7: Combining all the treatments results in our prototypical room.

What If?

There are always a lot of "what if" questions when you're dealing with real-world rooms that weren't purpose-designed to be recording studios and control rooms.

What if you have a window on the side wall next to your monitors?

▶ Hang a very heavy curtain over the window opening. (One source of heavy theater-style curtains is Rose Brand.)

▶ Create a "plug" that slips into the window opening. Cut a piece of wood or MDF (*medium density fiberboard*) to fit the opening. Cover the wood with fabric, mount acoustic foam or a glass fiber panel to the front, and slip it into the window opening.

Figure 9.8
One option for working with a window is to plug the opening with wood or MDF cut to fit, then cover the plug with acoustic foam or glass fiber panels.

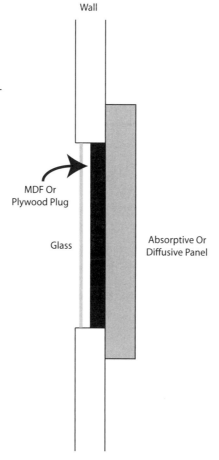

Wall

MDF Or
Plywood Plug

Glass

Absorptive Or
Diffusive Panel

▶ Mount acoustic foam or a glass fiber panel on a stand, then place it in front of the window opening. In the interest of symmetry, you might want to use a similar setup for the opposite wall as well.

▶ Hang a panel with glass fiber or foam over the window opening.

What if you have an opening or niche in a wall?

▶ Hang a heavy curtain over the opening.

▶ Use absorbers on stands to block the opening.

What if you have a door where you need to place treatment?

▶ Use flat hooks that hang over the top of the door to suspend the treatment material on the door surface. Mount the treatment to a thin sheet of wood, then hang the wood from wires off the hooks like a picture.

What if you can't put bass traps in all four corners?

▶ No problem; treat the corners that you can treat and leave the others alone. Symmetry is not as much of an issue with low-frequency treatment. If you need more bass trapping, treat the wall-to-ceiling corners.

CHAPTER 10

No-Budget Home Studio Plan

Don't have much of a budget for treating your studio acoustically? You can still put together a room that sounds very good! You're going to have to think creatively and use the materials you have available to you, but it can definitely be done.

Common Household Items

There are a variety of common items from around the house that you can use to help get your room's acoustical problems under control. There are a number of things that can serve as absorbers for your studio:

▶ Curtains and drapes work well. The heavier and softer the better—thin silk sheers aren't going to do the job. Don't hang them so tight that they're flat. Allow them to gather and fold to create extra depth. You can even hang a curtain as a canopy over the mix position to create a sort of cloud for helping with reflections off the ceiling. For better performance, use layers of heavy curtains for more absorption.

▶ Blankets and comforters, especially the heavy, soft type, can be hung just like curtains to provide absorption on walls and the ceiling. As with curtains, don't hang them flat; allow them to gather and fold.

▶ Pillows. It's hard to hang pillows on the wall, but set them around the room to help absorb stray high frequencies. It's going to take more than a couple of small throw pillows, so find as many as you can, as heavy and dense as possible. Try creating a pile of pillows on the floor in part of the room that can serve as an impromptu seating area when it's not sucking up sound.

▶ Bookcases. Load the shelves up with books for some diffusion. Or, as an alternative, stuff the shelves full of pillows, blankets, old clothes, anything soft you can find to create a big absorber you can place against a wall.

▶ Couches. Place a sofa, loveseat, or couch against one wall to help absorb some of the low end and to also help tame the reverberant decay in the room. If you can place more than one couch, even better!

▶ Chairs and ottomans. Hard wooden chairs or lightweight folding chairs aren't going to do much for us acoustically. But easy chairs, overstuffed loungers, a soft ottoman— all of these can help with low-end trapping and high-end absorption. Slide a soft chair or a solid ottoman into a corner to provide even more low-frequency control.

▶ Clothing. If you have a closet in the room, load it up with old clothes to create an effective bass trap.

▶ Room dividers. Those folding room dividers can be used to redirect reflections. Of course, you're going to need the type with solid panels in order for this to work. For even better results, cover the panels with something absorptive.

A Brand-New Plan

Let's take a look on the next page at the plan we came up with in the last chapter for placing acoustic treatments, but using our creatively sourced household materials to replace the commercial acoustic treatment products.

The principles for placing the treatments are the same as with commercial products; just substitute your home-grown materials as necessary. Nothing has changed as far as the need to treat first reflection points, to absorb low end to reduce the effects of room modes, and to bring reverberant decay and the evenness of the decay under control.

I'm not promising you'll get the same high-tech look you might get with commercial materials, or that the room's frequency response and decay time are going to be as good as with purpose-designed treatments, but you will get an improvement in the sound of your room. By putting your creativity to work, you can probably find a way to place these materials that will look just fine.

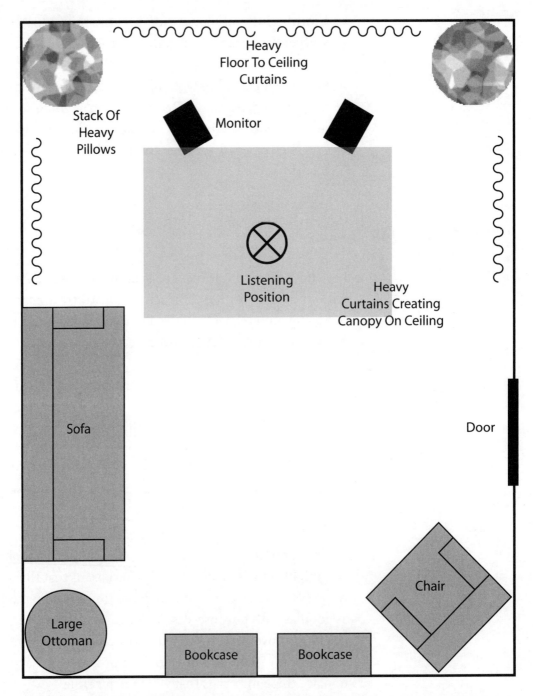

Figure 10.1: Creative substitution of household materials for commercial acoustical products can result in a good-sounding room that doesn't cost a fortune to treat.

And assuming you can steal—*errr*, borrow—some of these items from elsewhere in the house (do it quickly when your spouse isn't looking; he or she won't miss a sofa or some chairs from the living room) or pick them up inexpensively at yard sales or thrift stores, it won't cost much at all to completely treat your room.

CHAPTER 11

Fantasy Home Studio Plan

Now that we've looked at affordable acoustical treatment solutions and studio design, and even at an extremely low-budget solution to treating a room, let's take a look at the opposite end of the spectrum. Just what can you do when price is no object?

Okay, not many of us, short of scoring on the lottery, are ever going to be able to build a space even remotely like the one described in this chapter. But lest you think that this is just engaging in idle fantasy, there are practical reasons for including this way-over-the-top studio design. (And hey, what's wrong with the occasional idle fantasy?) For one, it's instructive to see how a top-tier professional acoustic designer/architect approaches designing a studio, and second, we can surely find some tips and tricks that we can steal!

Hiring a Designer

Working with a studio designer/architect is just like working with any other professional. You want to shop around and find someone who has a great track record, a great reputation, a respected portfolio of past work, and, perhaps most important of all, someone you can work with to find the right solutions to the design challenges your studio will face. You don't want someone who will dictate his or her ideas to you. Rather, you want someone to partner with you, take the time to understand your needs and wants, and to work with you.

As studio designer/architect Russ Berger told me:

> Recording studios and critical listening spaces have specialized functions and unique technical requirements that make them fundamentally different than other types of buildings. The design should be as future-proof as possible, creating spaces that can grow and adapt to changing needs. Sustainable concepts go hand-in-hand with these goals and are at the heart of intelligent design. A well-designed facility accommodates inevitable changes to the equipment complement, making updating and upgrading as easy as possible.
>
> Ultimately, it's not the ability of a design firm to address any one of these issues that makes them well suited to the job; it's their ability to handle all of these issues simultaneously, and to balance competing concerns. There are myriad details to

address, and the process will involve a series of choices and compromises in reconciling the issues of space, budget, function, quality, and schedule. There isn't just one way of creating the right space—the goal is to make the appropriate choices along the way. Having a depth of experience with similar facilities—and the ability to recognize how a facility is unique—gives studio designers confidence that the choices we make will be the right ones.

It definitely costs money to hire a studio designer. Still, to get a modest design done may not be as costly as you might think, especially if all you are after are drawings that you can work from to build the studio yourself. On the other end of the spectrum, you can hire the designer to handle the construction of your studio from the ground up—be prepared to shell out a few dollars if that's what you're after.

But if you're serious about your studio, it will be used for business and pleasure, and you have the means, a professional studio designer can take your studio in directions you might never have thought of on your own.

That was certainly the case here. I went to Russ Berger, president and namesake of Russ Berger Design Group (RBDG), and one of the most respected studio designers in the world (just check out some of his credits at www.rbdg.com) with a sketch of my home's walkout basement and the following requests:

▶ The studio should be large and open.

▶ The basement should have a home theater space as well as a recording space.

▶ I work with a lot of acoustic music, solo performers, and singer/songwriters, and I track electric guitars and similar instruments. I also do mixing, sound design, and composing in my studio.

▶ I'd like a nice place to practice steel-string and classical guitar.

▶ I don't do much full-on "band" recording at home—though I'd like to be able to if the need comes up. For serious drums or tracking a large or loud ensemble, I'm okay with renting time in a "commercial" studio.

▶ I wanted the full bath in the basement to remain.

▶ The view out the back of the basement looks onto a scenic pond and nature preserve. At least one window was a must.

On the following page you can see the sketch that I supplied to Russ, which shows the basement as it was when I moved into the house.

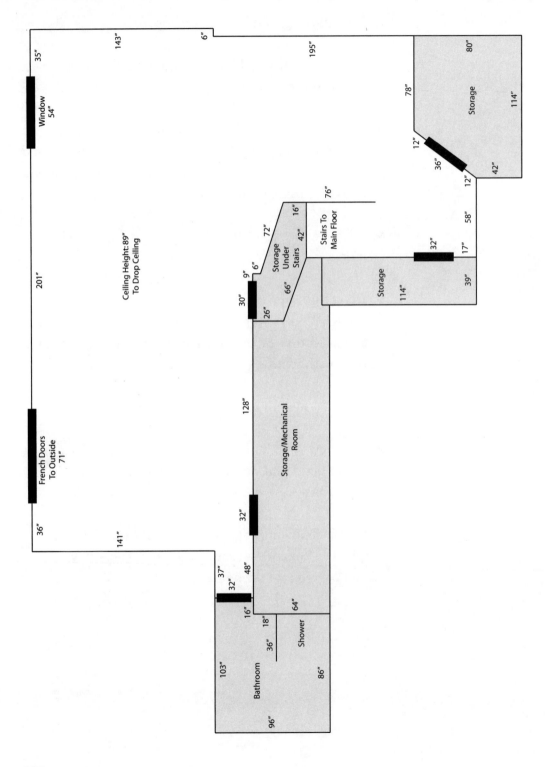

For a much-more cost-effective (and practical) solution to this design dilemma, turn to Chapter 15, "Studio Gallery: Basement." But read on to see what Russ came up with—it went beyond anything I expected (to say nothing of *way* beyond the capacity of my checkbook).

Russ Berger's plan for the basement, which you can see on the next page, includes a large dual-purpose control room/home theater (here configured for use as a control room; note the theater seats in the storage area), a large recording booth, a small office, even a small kitchenette. The "stage" area at the front of the control room can be put to use for recording artists, practicing, small group rehearsals, or even for intimate performances.

The view of Russ Berger's plan for the basement on page 105 shows the space configured as a home theater. The control surface/studio gear is rolled into the storage room, and the theater seats are placed to provide comfortable viewing.

The big feature of the new space is the dual-purpose control room/home theater. The gear and theater seats are set up to be mobile. When you're using the room as a studio, roll the theater seats out of the way, into the adjacent storage room. When you want to invite friends over and watch a movie, roll out the chairs and roll away the mixing console.

The large movie screen also does double-duty, serving as both a TV/movie screen and a computer display when you're working on a project. There's also a "stage"/ performance space, which opens up many opportunities for use of the space.

The absorption and diffusion required by both the recording booth and the control room are mostly built into the walls, which are then covered with fabric.

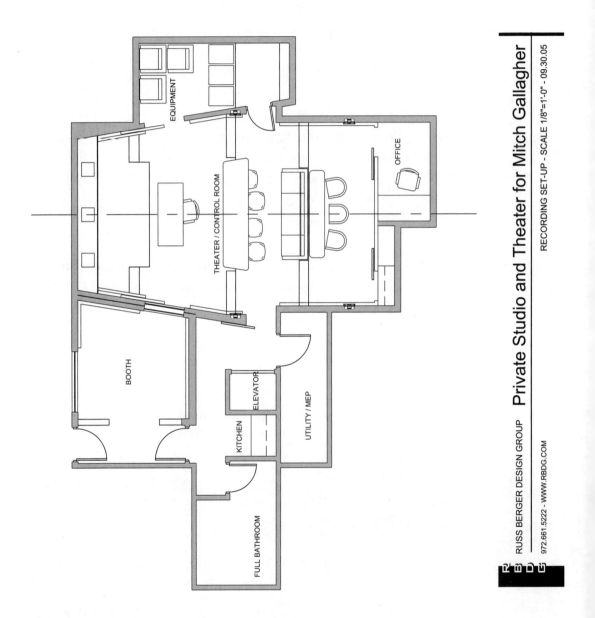

EQUIPMENT

OFFICE

THEATER / CONTROL ROOM

BOOTH

ELEVATOR

KITCHEN

UTILITY / MEP

FULL BATHROOM

RUSS BERGER DESIGN GROUP **Private Studio and Theater for Mitch Gallagher**

RECORDING SET-UP - SCALE 1/8"=1'-0" - 09.30.05

972.661.5222 - WWW.RBDG.COM

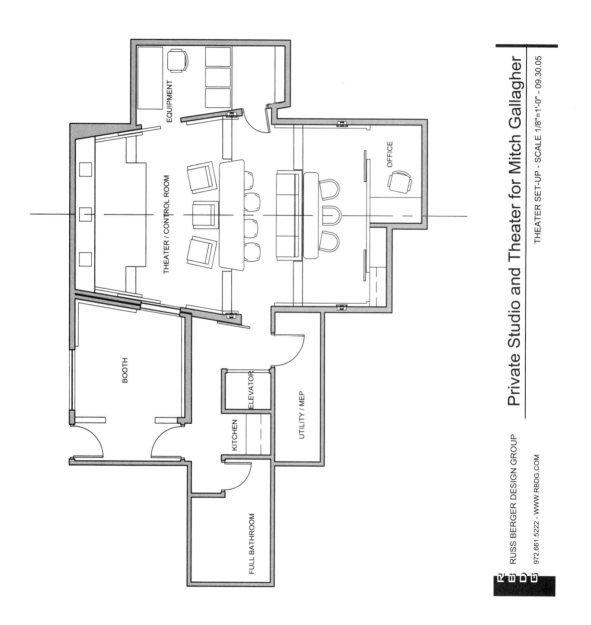

EQUIPMENT

THEATER / CONTROL ROOM

OFFICE

BOOTH

ELEVATOR

KITCHEN

UTILITY / MEP

FULL BATHROOM

Private Studio and Theater for Mitch Gallagher

THEATER SET-UP - SCALE 1/8"=1'-0" - 09.30.05

RUSS BERGER DESIGN GROUP

972.661.5222 - WWW.RBDG.COM

RBDG

The Designer's Notes

Russ Berger fills us in on the grand details:

This basement renovation concept combines a recording control room, studio, and equipment room with a music performance/rehearsal area and a home theater/screening room. It represents a successful series of compromises dictated by the function and the constraints of the space. While no budget constraints were placed on this renovation concept, efforts were made to be good stewards with Mitch's lottery money. Some of the features and functions may appear extreme to some, but they're based on cost-effective and proven methods, techniques, and concepts.

There are several overriding site constraints that have a significant impact on the layout. The basement area is currently limited to the footprint of the existing house and by severe height restrictions. In places we have expanded the basement to include areas outside of the footprint of the existing house.

Since there are no magic acoustical solutions that will overcome a lack of room volume, it was determined that the basement space should be lowered by digging out the floor. With a clear height of more than 14 feet, we can expect more accurate low-frequency response, better sight lines, and improved sound isolation.

The functional goals are best described by considering the whole as the sum of the rooms that make up the basement renovation. Access and egress from the basement is through an exterior door at the rear of the house to allow direct access for load in/out of equipment but ensuring a quiet, sound-isolated studio area. The existing stairs that lead to the house's main floor take up considerable space, are not conveniently located in the traffic flow pattern, and have been replaced in this plan with a residential elevator. This has the added benefit of controlling access to the residential spaces above from clients gone on "walk-about."

In a matter of minutes, the main critical-listening space can be transformed from a recording control room, to a performance/rehearsal space, to a screening room/home theater. The room is configured to provide multi-channel surround audio for groups of people, regardless of whether the group is there to record or to enjoy entertainment. Sliding acoustical vision panels located on either side at the front of the control room/theater will help optimize the listening and performance conditions by taming specular reflections.

The video presentation is optimized for screening product and entertainments. A high-resolution projector is housed at the rear of the room in a sound-isolation enclosure. A multi-image video processor will support full-screen images or subdivide the screen into as many as 16 individual images in multi-formats. For example, when the room is in a recording configuration, the screen can be divided into a large area for a computer-driven Pro Tools/DAW display, a separate screen area for playback of high-definition (HD) video, security cameras from the front and back door, an Internet browser window, and the football game currently in progress. Each individual window on the screen can be relocated and resized to match user preferences.

When configured as a screening theater, three tiers of "A-ticket" seats will provide groups of eight to twelve people with excellent surround audio and unencumbered visual sightlines. A combination of commercial-quality fixed seats, soft seating (movable armchairs), and floor pillows provides flexibility and ensures optimum listening location and conditions. Chairs can be moved about and reconfigured to accommodate guest preferences, or the chairs can be removed from the room entirely. A stage area at the front of the control room/theater will accommodate soloists and small ensembles performing with acoustic or light electric instrumentation. These performances can be recorded or enjoyed by people sitting in the theater space.

Most spaces dedicated to rehearsal or practice are small in size and sound, physically cramping the performer and constraining the sonic performance of the space. Compared with an adequately sized room, acoustically small rooms typically require more sound-absorption materials to tame unpleasant resonance.

To help overcome this common error of over-treating a room with absorption, diffusors and distributed absorption are combined with a substantial volume of 6,200 cubic feet to support the performance area. Performances from the raised stage area will be enjoyed from tiered seating in optimized listening positions and with excellent sight lines.

Even though the space is significantly larger than that set aside for most practice environments, there will be little ambience or room character to support and enhance the performers' musical efforts. A LARES assisted reverberation system, a system that we [Russ Berger Design Group] helped implement and integrate into the Wenger V-Room practice environment and other performance environments, is incorporated into both the control room/theater and the studio/booth space.

The LARES assisted reverberation system [www.lares-lexicon.com] will provide acoustic enhancement for performances by electronically emulating rooms considerably larger in volume. The system will simulate the sound of performance venues ranging in size from a small club to a concert hall.

Performers and the audience will hear the acoustic response of a much larger and specially treated acoustic space. The LARES system has the side benefit of offering superior surround theater performance as well.

Theater gear, amplifiers, outboard gear, and recording control surfaces will be housed in an adjacent equipment area, part of the basement expansion. Additional signal-processing gear is conveniently placed and easily accessed in a low credenza to support the recording process, yet is discretely concealed behind the first row of seating when the room is in theater mode.

On one side at the rear of the control room/screening theater, a concealed storage area houses media and supplies. The other side conceals access to a small office space with a desk and built-ins.

The studio [recording booth] will provide a quiet, sound-isolated environment that is specially treated to support music performance and recording. Access to the studio from the rest of the basement is provided through a sound-rated door, opening onto the connecting corridor that leads to the control room. The studio's volumetric relationship is optimized for smooth low-frequency response. An acoustical window, constructed from multiple panes of 3/4-inch sound-rated laminated glass, runs from floor to 7 feet high and provides sight lines between the talent and the control room. Sloped low-frequency traps flanking the two entry doors improve low-frequency performance and help define the entrance. A large sound-rated exterior window with motorized shades draws natural light through the studio and into all of the adjoining spaces.

The existing utility room will be relocated as part of the basement expansion into an adjacent area. This space will house the multi-zoned HVAC [heating and cooling] system for the basement studio and control areas, lighting dimmers, the technical power and grounding system, as well as utilities for the remainder of the residence. A kitchen/pantry area is located along a wide spot in the connecting corridor and includes a sink, small refrigerator, dishwasher, and wood-burning pizza oven. (Just kidding about the pizza oven!) A bathroom with shower is located at the end of the connecting corridor beyond the pantry.

Radiant heating will be incorporated into floor finishes that will include wood with stone accents. Wall finishes will include a combination of gypsum wallboard, masonry, wood, and custom field-fabricated fabric systems with environmentally sustainable acoustical core materials. Lighting will be a mixture of incandescent and full-spectrum LED accents controlled with remote dimming and color selection systems.

Pretty wild transformation! After looking over Russ's plans, I couldn't resist, I just had to know: How much?

Russ replied (after stifling his laughter): "How much? [*more laughter*] Seriously, that's the wrong question. The right question is, 'How soon can I have it?' [*still more laughter*] Considering the cost of construction in your area, probably $350k to finish out the shell space as designed. However, digging out under a house can get expensive…add maybe an additional $100k to make the shell ready and to relocate the utilities. Kinda puts a crimp in the old lunch money for the next few years…."

But even those figures don't include furniture, electronics, architect's and engineer's fees, etc., etc., etc. Plan on dropping a cool million for the complete rebuild and remodeling of the basement.

Why You Should Care

Okay, so maybe Russ' design is a few dollars over most of our budgets. But what can we, who live in the real world financially, learn from this little fantasy exercise? There are several important things we can apply to our studios.

1. Rooms can serve more than one purpose. No one says your studio has to just be a studio. Because it's acoustically treated, it might also make a great home theater, music listening room, or practice/rehearsal space.

2. Equipment doesn't have to stay in one spot. With careful planning and creative wiring, a mixing desk or

control surface can roll right out of the way, giving you space for doing other things.

3. Equipment can serve multiple purposes. A high-definition television, for example, can play movies and TV shows and serve as a monitor for your computer.

4. Nothing is fixed in place. You can change walls and even floors if you want to (and can afford to have it done).

5. Good acoustical performance and architecture can coexist, enhancing the experience of each. A good-looking, well-planned room always sounds a little better and can surely do more to inspire your best work.

6. Think outside the box. Take a fresh look at your space. If you do so, new ideas may occur to you. Though my studio is finished (Chapter 15), Russ Berger's design has given me several ideas for more effectively using the space. Maybe I can't afford to dig out floors to gain more ceiling height or expand the basement, but I can consider relocating or reorienting my studio or combining it with a home theater.

That's it for our trip to fantasyland. Let's get our feet back on the ground and continue on with our quest for a better-sounding studio.

CHAPTER 12

Noise Control

As you treat your studio and it sounds better and better, you're going to have the aural clarity to notice details in your recordings that you never heard before. In some cases you'll hear good things, but often you'll hear problems—distortion you didn't notice before, too much reverb, muddiness, all sorts of things. While it's disappointing to find problems in recordings and mixes that you slaved over, ultimately it's a good thing. Once you can hear the problems, you can get to work and fix them.

You'll also start to notice other things as your room improves: environmental noise such as computer fans, hard drive noise, heating and air conditioning noise, outside noise, and more.

Equipment Noise

Reducing the noise floor in your studio will let you hear what's coming out of your monitors much better—the monitors won't be fighting to be heard over the background noise. Fortunately, taming equipment noise isn't too difficult.

Most studios these days are computer-based, and that means fan noise. Some computers are quieter than others, so the first thing you can do is to switch to a less noisy machine. There are computers that are specially designed and configured for the lowest possible noise. I've tested some of these machines, and they are so quiet you can actually record near them with little noise bleed. Sweetwater's Creation Station series is one of the quietest of those I've used.

If you can't afford to or don't want to purchase a new computer, you can look at quieting your computer down with lower-noise fans, liquid cooling systems, sound-insulated cases, or other methods.

Another solution is to house your computer and other noisy gear, such as hard drives, in an isolation cabinet. Companies such as Sound Construction & Supply and Raxxess manufacture nicely finished units, which are enclosed racks with built-in quiet fans, temperature monitoring, glass doors, and other features.

If you're moderately handy, you can build an enclosure yourself for your computer. Line the enclosure with acoustic foam or other absorption, and be sure to allow for ventilation. Low-speed, quiet fans can be used, or you can cut vent holes in the cabinet to release some heat—computers do need a source of fresh air in order to stay cool.

For my last studio, I built a very simple isolation box—essentially a big cubical box made from MDF (*medium-density fiberboard*) with hinged front and rear doors, and ventilation holes in the back, as well as a slot in the bottom to let cables pass in and out. To keep the computer as cool as possible, I kept the box's doors ajar when I wasn't recording or doing critical listening. When I was doing something critical, I'd close the doors tightly. Not fancy, but it worked surprisingly well. (I can't stress enough how important it is to make sure your computers and drives don't overheat!)

If your studio is located in a bedroom, there may be a handy closet where you can place your computer and hard drives. Run any necessary cables under the door. This is what I'm doing in my current studio—the computers are in a nearby storage closet now dubbed "The Machine Room." I did have to purchase monitor and keyboard/mouse extension cables, but the expense was worth it to get the noisy machines out of the control room. (You could also use a wireless keyboard and mouse.)

If you have an adjacent room to the studio, you may be able to drill small holes through the wall to run cables through, and place the computer next door. Pack the holes around the cables with acoustic foam or fluffy glass fiber to seal them as well as possible. This solution is ideal because the computer and drives will remain well ventilated in the next-door room, yet you won't have to listen to and work around fan noise. Just make sure you know what you're doing when you drill or cut through the wall—you don't want to hit a water line or electric cable. (A big mess and potentially very dangerous as well...be careful!) Of course, before you start drilling or cutting the wall, make sure that your computer will be safe and out of the way in the room next door!

Whatever you do to quiet your computer down, be sure that you provide adequate ventilation to keep the machine's operating temperature well down in the safe range. Heat will destroy a computer or hard drive very quickly!

HVAC

Heating, Ventilation, and Air Conditioning (HVAC) is an essential component of any home or project studio—things get pretty uncomfortable without heating or air conditioning, and a sealed studio gets unbearable quickly without adequate ventilation. The problem is that most HVAC systems aren't designed with minimum noise production in mind. Ducts vibrate and resonate, airflow rushes through vents, fans blow and make noise.

The bad news is that to retrofit a quieter system into an existing space is a fairly monumental undertaking—to say nothing of the fact that a new HVAC system could run $10,000 or even much more. What's involved are flexible ducts that don't resonate, large diameter plumbing and ducts to reduce air speed while maintaining air volume, custom venting, quiet fans, and more. All in all, a major deal, and not one that's very doable for most home and project studios.

So can you do anything to help with HVAC noise and to help prevent sound from entering the HVAC system in the studio and being heard elsewhere in the house or building?

More bad news. There's probably not much that can be done with your existing HVAC system. To prevent noise from the studio from getting into the system, you can build covers to slip over the vent openings when you are making noise. You could also install doors that close over the vent openings.

As far as stopping noise from the HVAC system, the only really affordable solution I've found is to turn off the air conditioning or heating when you are tracking or doing critical listening. It's a pain in the summer because audio gear generates a ton of heat, but it works. It's the solution I use in my home studio.

Another option worth investigating: I haven't used it myself, but others recommend "Mr. Slim" from Mitsubishi. This stand-alone HVAC unit is said to be very quiet and requires only a small hole through the wall for the coolant line. For more information, see http://www. mitsubishielectric.com.sg/aircon/pc.asp.

CHAPTER 13

Sound Isolation

Our goal in this tome isn't to dig too deeply into soundproofing…or to be more politically correct, "sound isolation." Most true solutions to keeping sound contained within a space or preventing sound from entering a space require pretty serious construction and use of a variety of materials. Still, it may be useful to understand some of the concepts of isolation. More importantly, we'll look at a few things you can do to reduce the bleed of noise either into or out of your studio.

If you're building your space from the ground up, building a room-within-a-room design, or gutting a space and rebuilding it, it's possible to construct walls and ceilings that greatly help with keeping sound that's inside the room inside, and sound that's outside the room outside.

Keep It Down in There

We're not here to study construction, but following are some of the techniques that are used in building sound-isolated rooms:

▶ "Float" the floor of the room on hard rubber pucks, then build the walls and ceiling on top of the floating floor.

▶ Use a "sandwich" technique to build the walls: a layer of gypsum wallboard, a layer of limp mass sound barrier, a layer of gypsum wallboard, and so on.

Figure 13.1
Using a "sandwich" of different materials for the walls is one technique for creating better isolation.

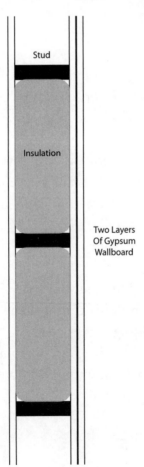

Stud

Insulation

Two Layers
Of Gypsum
Wallboard

▶ Hang gypsum wallboard from a resilient channel rather than screwing it straight to the studs; this is sort of like mounting the wall surfaces to a spring or shock absorber.

▶ Use double-wall construction. Two walls are constructed next to each other, separated by an air space.

Figure 13.2
Two walls separated by an air space provide excellent isolation.

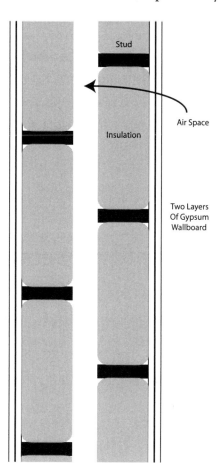

Stud

Air Space

Insulation

Two Layers
Of Gypsum
Wallboard

▶ Seal everything—for this application, caulking is your friend. Any space that air can get through will allow sound to get through.

► Avoid making holes in the walls to mount electrical outlets, lighting fixtures, light switch boxes, and so on. Instead, surface-mount those and other items on the walls and ceiling.

► Stuff walls and ceiling full of fluffy glass fiber.

► Use mass. It takes heavy material to stop powerful low frequencies. Extra layers of gypsum wallboard, heavy plywood, and so on. Note that this method of isolation will result in the most change to the room's acoustics. Heavy mass will keep more low-frequency energy inside the room, preventing it from escaping. This in turn will make any modal problems that much worse. There's no way around this tradeoff—better sound isolation means more energy in the room, which means the acoustic problems get worse. So using this technique will mean that you have to step up your treatments in the room as well.

► Install the quietest, most noise-resistant HVAC system available.

► Use double-pane, laminated, sound-rated glass for windows.

► Use sound-rated doors—possibly even two doors hung back to back on the same jamb or separated by an air space.

The list goes on, and it quickly gets expensive if you really want to completely isolate your space from the rest of the world.

So What Can You Do without Building?

Unfortunately, not many of the items on the preceding list are applicable to an existing room in a house or building, especially if budget is a serious consideration. So what can you do to help isolate your studio?

DISTANCE

Sound obeys the inverse-square law, which says that intensity is inversely proportional to the square of the distance. The inverse-square law applies to gravitational force, light brightness, radiation intensity, electric fields, and more. In regard to acoustics, the inverse-square law works based on the fact that sound energy leaving a point source spreads out. Sound energy twice a given distance from a point source spreads out over four times the area. So every time you double the distance, the sound has one-fourth the intensity. It works the same at other distances; three times the distance has one-ninth the intensity. Ten times the distance has 1/100th the intensity.

This works out to a 6 dB drop every time you double the distance; 10 times the distance reduces loudness by 20 dB. You can use this to your advantage. The more distance you can put between you and any listeners you might potentially annoy, or between you and any noise that might bleed into your recordings, the better. And the farther away you can locate noisy items such as computers and hard drives, the better.

WALLS AND CEILINGS

It takes mass to stop low-frequency waves from getting into or out of your studio. If you're dealing with a room that's already been constructed, you may be limited as to what you can do. If you're willing to remodel the room, you could add an additional layer of gypsum wallboard, add a layer of plywood to the floor, add gypsum wallboard to the ceiling, and so on. Lots of work, though. And for naught, unless you follow through and beef up the entire room—sound isolation is only as good as the weakest link.

DOORS

There are several things you can do to improve the sound isolation of the door(s) in your room. The first is to make sure the door seals tightly against the frame by installing a gasket or weather stripping. If you want to get serious, you can look into drop seals that mount to the bottom of the door. These seals drop down when the door is closed so that the air gap at the bottom of the door is plugged. For maximum isolation, you could elect to replace the door with a sound-rated door, though this will be pricey.

WINDOWS

Windows are almost always a weak link in the sound isolation—regular glass passes low and low-mid frequencies easily. You could replace the pane(s) with laminated sound-rated glass or replace the entire window with a sound-rated window. If you're looking for a "non-destructive" option where you don't have to spend much money or make any permanent modifications, construct a "plug" of 3/4" MDF or plywood that slides snugly into the window opening. Cover it with acoustic treatment, and you have a pretty good solution—though not one that passes sunlight very well. But if you need to let the sun shine in or to open the window for ventilation, you can always temporarily pull the plug out of the window frame.

Reality Sets In

Ultimately, complete sound isolation is difficult and expensive. And it's often beyond the scope of what we can do in home and project studios. If you're after the best isolation with the least investment, the best bet is to place your studio in the basement, where you only have to worry about the floor overhead. Insulate heavily, double-up the gypsum wallboard on the ceiling, seal everything up tightly, and call it a day.

If you don't have a basement, you don't have the funds necessary for a remodel, and you're not inclined to make modifications to your house or building, you'll likely have to live with what you've got…though at least consider making plugs for the windows and sealing the doors with weather stripping.

Without sound isolation, you'll need to exercise some care and courtesy when recording and mixing. For maximizing the neighborhood peace quotient, when you must make loud noise, do it when no one is sleeping and when the neighbors won't be disturbed. If you're recording quiet, delicate instruments, do it when there won't be much noise in the house or outside. For me, this means tracking fingerpicked acoustic guitar late at night, when the rest of the house is asleep and the neighborhood is quiet. Not a big deal, really, and much easier and certainly much less expensive than real sound isolation!

Part III

Studio Gallery

· · · · · · · · · · · ·

Welcome to the *Acoustic Design for the Home Studio* gallery. In the following pages, you'll find four home studios—real rooms in real houses—as well as a "machine room" designed to isolate noisy studio equipment, such as computers and hard drives, and a small recording booth (again, all real rooms). Each chapter will detail an approach for treating its particular room for much-improved acoustic response.

What is important here isn't the specifics of the rooms presented; what is important is the concepts used to treat the problems in those rooms: how reflections and flutter echo are handled, how reverberant decay is controlled, and how low-frequency response is shaped. So while you probably won't find a room here that exactly matches the room you'll be using for your studio, you'll hopefully see a plan that is at least similar enough that you are able to apply the concepts to your own space.

As mentioned above, these are all real rooms. In some cases, we've even performed acoustical analysis of the space before and after treatment so that we can examine the effectiveness of the concepts we've been discussing. (Special thanks to Auralex Acoustics, and in particular Auralex Chief Acoustical Engineer Jeff Szymanski, for help with analyzing the rooms and creating the various graphs.)

CHAPTER 14

Studio Gallery: Home Office

This room is a general-purpose space located just off the house's family room. Previously the space had been used as a home office. The room is a basic rectangle, with hard gypsum wallboard walls and ceiling, and a hardwood floor. There are two doors and one window.

The dimensions for the room are 14 feet long by a bit over 9 feet wide by 8 feet high. The room was, with all those parallel hard surfaces, predictably very live. Flutter echo wasn't a huge problem (though it was there). The big problem was reverberant decay. Clapping your hands in the room created a sound like smacking the side of a basketball.

*Figure 14.1
The home office room,
without any treatments or
furnishings.*

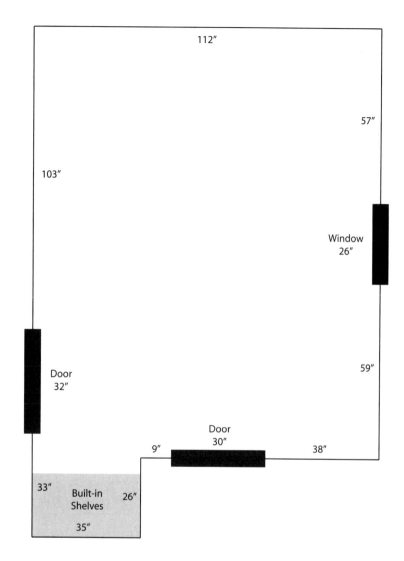

Looking at the room, we're going to orient the studio such that it "fires" the long way in the space, so the speakers aim toward the door in the short wall behind you. This allows us to place the speakers in the symmetrical end of the room and take advantage of the longer length of the room, while keeping the asymmetrical part of the studio behind the main listening position.

Figure 14.2
The former home office, now a functional recording studio with well-controlled first reflections and bass trapping.

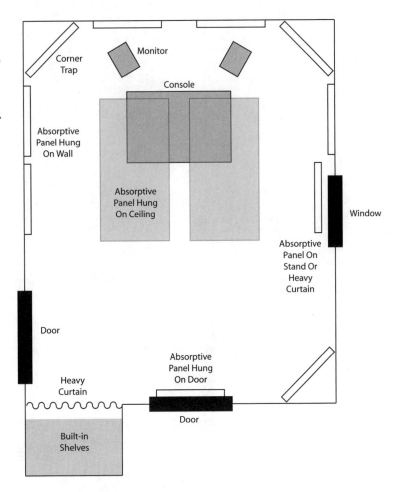

Low Frequencies

The first order of business is to take care of the bottom end. Low frequencies will be shaped using 2-foot by 4-foot absorptive panels placed across the three open room corners to create broadband absorbers covering the corners from floor to ceiling. In the remaining corner, there are shelves built across a small alcove in the room. While these shelves will obviously be useful for storage, they can be put to another use as well: as bass traps. Stuff the top shelf full of absorption (either cut rigid glass fiber panels or acoustic foam panels to fit or use fluffy glass fiber) from the shelf to the ceiling, filling the entire space. Stuff the area below the bottom shelf in the same way. If you've used glass fiber to stuff the two shelf areas, cover the openings with cloth to prevent fibers from getting out into the room. If you don't need the shelving, stuff the remaining two shelves as well for even more low-frequency control.

Figure 14.3
By stuffing the top shelf and the area below the bottom shelf with absorption, those areas of the alcove at the rear of the studio become effective bass traps.

Stuff this area full of absorptive material and cover with fabric

Stuff this area full of absorptive material and cover with fabric

If you're not filling all the shelves with absorption, hang a heavy curtain in front of the shelves to hide the inevitable clutter and to provide more absorptive area on the rear wall. By letting the curtain gather up, rather than hanging it stretched tight so it's flat, we'll get a small amount of diffusion in the highest frequencies.

REFLECTIONS

First reflection control will be handled by 2-foot by 4-foot absorptive panels on the walls on both sides of the room. On the left side (as you face the monitors), the panels can be hung on the wall. Use a mirror to find the ideal location, as described in Chapter 9. If you'll be working primarily seated, place the panels centered height-wise on the wall. (They'll extend from two feet from the floor to six feet from the floor.) If you or the musicians you work with will be standing—vocalists, for example—you may want to hang the panels slightly higher.

On the right side, one panel can be hung on the wall, but there won't be room for the second to hang because of the location of the window. There are several options.

1. You could opt to hang a heavy curtain over the window instead of an absorptive panel. Although this is an easy option, the curtain probably won't perform as well acoustically as a panel would.

2. Mount an absorptive panel to a light backing board, mount the backing board on a stand (a straight microphone stand may work, or you can make a simple stand from tubing or wood), then position the stand in front of the window.

3. Hang an absorptive panel vertically from the ceiling, in front of the window. Simply put hooks in the ceiling, mount the absorptive panel to a backing board, and

suspend the backing board from a wire (or wires) at the desired height.

4. Plug the window with 3/4-inch MDF or plywood, then cover the wooden plug with a 2-foot by 4-foot absorptive panel. This will make the two walls the most alike, but at the expense of losing easy access to the window.

Personally, I've worked in enough cave-like studios that I place a great deal of value on an outside view and the ability to let the sun shine in. For this reason, I prefer either option 1 or option 2, which still allow easy access to the window. You may also be able to utilize option 3 and still have access to the window—just reach up and unhook the panel when you want to let the great outdoors in for a visit.

First reflections from the ceiling will be handled with two 2-foot by 4-foot absorptive panels. These can either be mounted right to the surface of the ceiling or suspended a few inches down on hooks and wires (which will help to increase the low-frequency performance of the panel). Reflections from the rear wall will be handled by a 2-foot by 4-foot absorptive panel mounted to the door.

OPTIONS

For even more low-frequency/broadband absorption, you could also place 2-foot by 4-foot absorptive panels at 45 degrees across the wall-to-ceiling corners. This will increase the broadband absorption in the room substantially. In fact, with all the absorption already in place, this additional amount may make the room too dead. If this is the case, consider using glass fiber panels with metallic backing to restore some high-frequency life to the room.

If you will be recording musicians standing or sitting in the rear of the room, behind the mix position, consider placing two more 2-foot by 4-foot absorptive panels over that location as well. In this situation, you may also want more absorption on the walls in the rear of the room, but take care not to completely deaden the room.

CHAPTER 15

Studio Gallery: Basement

Unless you skipped reading everything up to this point, you've seen this chapter's room before. It's the same walkout basement that was completely transformed into a studio fantasyland by studio designer/architect Russ Berger in Chapter 11. This time, however, we're going to take a much more down-to-earth approach to creating a workable space. If you've forgotten what the room looked like, the next page shows a refresher of the space without any furnishings or acoustic treatment.

In this chapter we'll be focusing on just the main area of the room. In later chapters we'll be converting one storage room into a recording booth, and the storage space under the stairs into a machine room for isolating computers and other noisy equipment.

Before I placed any treatment in the room, I experimented a bit with the layout. I wanted the space to serve multiple functions:

▶ As a control room area for the studio

▶ As a space for practicing classical and steel-string acoustic guitar

▶ As a home theater/entertainment area

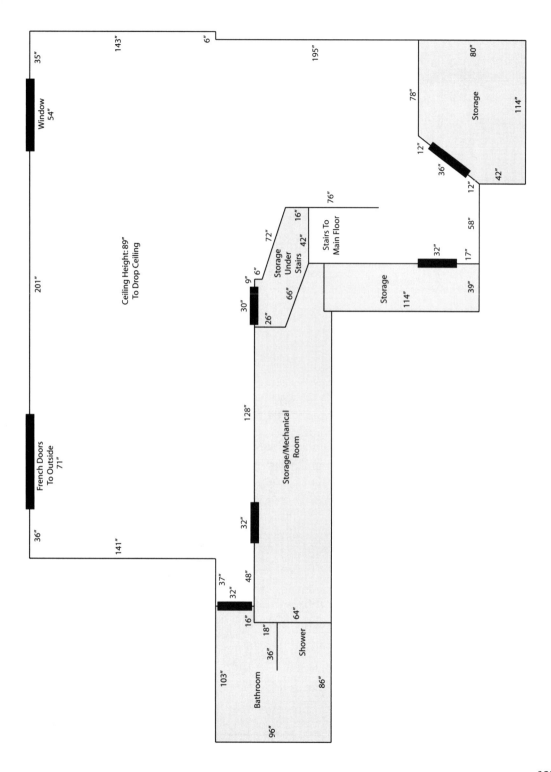

35"

143"

6"

195"

80"

Window
54"

78"

Storage

201"

114"

12"

36"

Ceiling Height: 89"
To Drop Ceiling

42"

12"

76"

16"

58"

72"

Storage
Under
Stairs

Stairs To
Main Floor

9" 6"

42"

30"

32"

26"

66"

17"

Storage

39"

128"

114"

French Doors
To Outside
71"

Storage/Mechanical
Room

32"

36"

37"

141"

32"

48"

16"

18"

64"

36"

Shower

103"

86"

Bathroom

96"

Where to Go?

Because this is an L-shaped room, there are a number of places where the studio could be placed. It would seem to make the most sense to place the studio so that the monitors were in the area near the French doors, firing down the long leg of the L. And acoustically, this may be the ideal location. But after temporarily setting the gear up in that location, the studio ended up in the way of the traffic path from the French doors and was also encroaching on the traffic path to the full bathroom at the end of the basement.

Figure 15.1:

This placement was problematic because of traffic flow in the room.

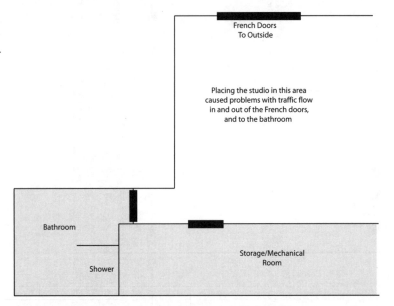

Placed in the small area of the L, the studio interfered with the traffic flow from the stairs. And the asymmetrical shape of that part of the room was a problem for placing treatment—compounded by the need to place the studio off to one side in order for the traffic to get through unimpeded. The effects of the asymmetrical room shape were easy to hear, making this location unacceptable.

Figure 15.2
There was nowhere in this
part of the room that worked
well for placing the studio—
traffic flow and asymmetry
were big problems.

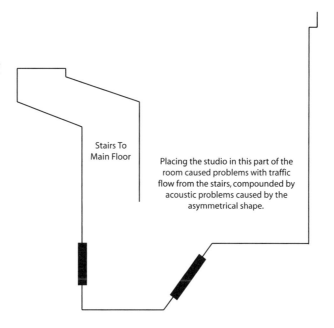

Stairs To
Main Floor

Placing the studio in this part of the
room caused problems with traffic
flow from the stairs, compounded by
acoustic problems caused by the
asymmetrical shape.

I also tried the studio at the junction of the L, but the asymmetrical shape once again caused problems with treatment placement and created an audible difference between the left and right sides when listening.

Figure 15.3
The corner area of the L-
shaped room didn't work well;
the asymmetry was a very
audible problem.

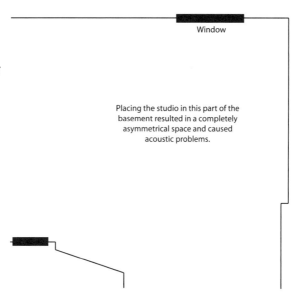

Window

Placing the studio in this part of the
basement resulted in a completely
asymmetrical space and caused
acoustic problems.

In the end, I placed the studio in the middle of the long leg of the L, so the listener faced toward the wall with the window and French doors. There are several advantages to this position:

▶ It's as far as possible from the side walls, resulting in little problem from first reflections coming off those surfaces. The distance to the side walls is well over 10 feet, so first reflections return to the listening position long after 20ms—outside where they would cause significant difficulties.

▶ The asymmetrical aspects of the room are behind the listener.

▶ The storage area under the stairs is conveniently located for use as an isolation room for computers and other noisy equipment. (See Chapter 19, "Studio Gallery: Machine Room.")

▶ There's a great view out the French doors and the window. As mentioned in the last chapter, I'm willing to compromise a bit in order to have a window in the studio. But in this case, with this location there was no real acoustical compromise necessary.

▶ The home theater can be set up to the side of the studio, so the television can be easily seen from the main work positions. (Nice for long, tedious editing sessions....) Plus, musicians and/or clients can relax on the sofa during the session.

▶ The studio doesn't interfere with the traffic flow down the stairs, to the bathroom, or in or out of the French doors.

▶ There's a nice area for practicing guitar at the end of the room opposite the theater area, in front of the French doors.

▶ The area adjacent to the stairs can be used for other purposes—family entertainment, as a recording space, or whatever.

▶ The large storage room at the bottom of the stairs can be easily made into a recording booth. (See Chapter 18, "Studio Gallery: Recording Booth.")

▶ The other storage room at the bottom of the stairs can be used for storing microphones and microphone stands, guitar amps, software manuals, cables, and other studio essentials.

The negative with this studio placement is the relatively short distance from the listening position to the back wall. But in listening tests, the effects of this weren't significant (especially after treating the room). The asymmetrical location of the short leg of the room behind and to the right of the listener is also a negative. But after listening to the room, the decision was made to leave that part of the room alone. If the extra ambience from that space becomes problematic, there are several solutions: Movable absorptive panels on stands could be placed across the opening, a heavy curtain could be hung across the opening to close off the space, or the room itself could be treated with absorption.

After experimenting with several locations for the studio in the basement, this layout emerged as the most workable solution. All the requirements of the room are met, and only a minimum of treatment will be required. Figures 15.4 through 15.6 show how the room looked before treatment. Page 144 shows the way the final room layout came together.

Figure 15.4
Looking toward the French
doors. To the top of the
picture, in front of the two
bookcases, is the acoustic gui-
tar practice area. (Photo by
David Stewart.)

Figure 15.5
From the storage closet under the stairs (which later became the machine room), looking toward the front of the studio area. (Photo by David Stewart.)

Figure 15.6
Looking toward the back of the room. (Photo by David Stewart.)

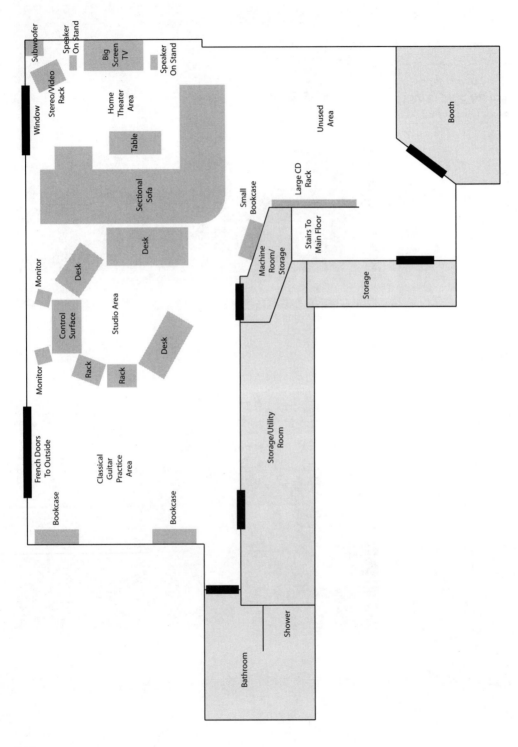

To create a benchmark for the effectiveness of the treatments applied, three frequency sweeps were recorded in the room—one at the engineer's listening position; another behind the engineer, where the producer or musician would be located; and the third against the rear wall. The mid- and high-frequency results were encouraging; there were no serious problems. A few peaks would need to be addressed with a bit of absorption on the front and back walls, but the side walls would not need to be addressed. Listening tests verified this—the highs and mids were surprisingly true. The low-frequency portion of the sweeps was analyzed, resulting in the graph shown in Figure 15.7. Notice the range of levels for the engineer's listening position—nearly 50 dB from the highest peak to the lowest dip. Our goal will be to substantially reduce this spread and to even out the overall response.

Clearly there were some modes at work, but the results weren't bad. This is probably due to the size of the room and the fact that there is only a single sheet of gypsum wallboard between the studio area and the storage/mechanical room; low frequencies will pass right through such an inconsequential barrier. The result is that at low frequencies, the two spaces almost function as one.

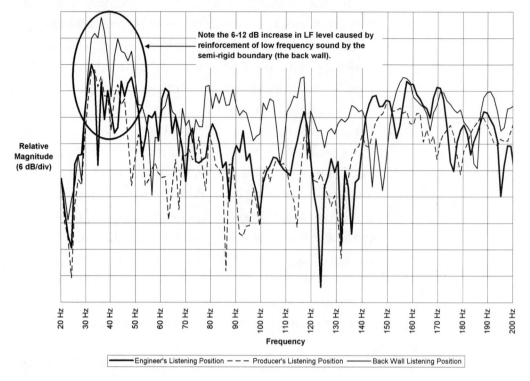

Figure 15.7: Low-frequency response of the control room area before application of any acoustic treatments. (Courtesy of Auralex Acoustics, Inc.)

This basement space will actually be treated quite simply, as you'll see on the following page: Broadband absorption is the order of the day.

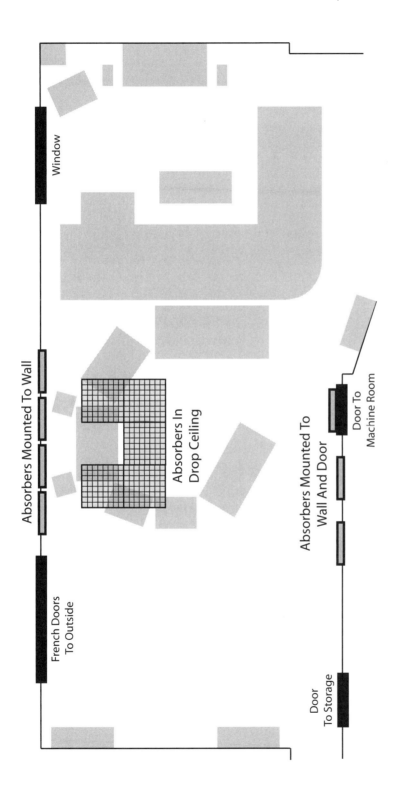

Low Frequencies

We began by treating the low frequencies. Because there were no nearby corners, we decided to utilize the space above the drop ceiling for bass trapping. There was about 5 inches clear above the ceiling tiles; above that were the joists supporting the floor above, which were stuffed with rolled out glass fiber.

We wanted to replace the ceiling tiles immediately above the mix position—those that were in the path of first reflections—because the existing tiles had a hard surface that was reflecting back midrange and high frequencies and also interacting with the floor, which is simply carpet on concrete (no carpet pad). Any type of absorption could have been used to replace the ceiling tiles. The ceiling grid had 2-foot by 2-foot openings, so rigid glass fiber panels cut to size could have been used, as could acoustic foam or another, more absorptive type of ceiling tile. (Be careful when choosing ceiling tiles—the acoustic performance of some types is far better than others. If in doubt, ask to see the NRC and absorption coefficients for the tile before buying.)

In the end, we used a new product called a "SpaceCoupler" from Auralex Acoustics that acts almost like a lens, redirecting acoustic waves. To improve absorption, the SpaceCouplers were covered with SonoFiber, an absorptive material. Where possible, we doubled or tripled the SonoFiber for better low-frequency performance. Interestingly, the SpaceCouplers also provide some diffusion because sound striking the unit is broken up and redirected. Figure 15.8 shows how Auralex SpaceCouplers topped with absorption were used to redirect sound waves and to provide low-frequency control. The absorption on top was made as thick as possible to provide maximum low-frequency performance. The surrounding joists were filled with rolled-out glass fiber insulation.

Figure 15.8
Auralex SpaceCouplers topped with absorption were used to redirect sound waves and to provide low-frequency control. (Photo by David Stewart.)

Figure 15.9 shows how five ceiling tiles were replaced with new treatment. The center panel in the tiles above the listening position couldn't be replaced because there was an HVAC duct above it—when you're dealing with an existing space, you're inevitably going to run into some restrictions to what you can do. Still, the U-shaped treatment arrangement thankfully fell perfectly for solving the ceiling's first-reflection problems.

Figure 15.9
Five ceiling tiles were replaced
with new treatment. (Photo
by David Stewart.)

The results of this treatment were excellent. The graph in Figure 15.10 shows the low-frequency response before and after the ceiling was treated. The "before" response is the bottom graph; the "after" is the top. The range of variation went from 52 dB (±26 dB) to 34 dB (±17 dB)—a substantial improvement in the low end, with a minimal amount of treatment.

As important as the improvement in frequency response is the smoothing the treatment provided for low-frequency reverberant decay as shown in Figure 15.11.

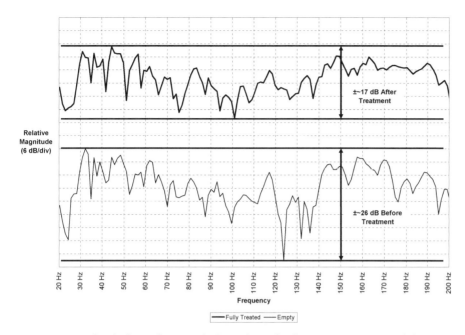

Figure 15.10: This before/after graph shows how the frequency response of the space was shaped using treatment in the ceiling. (Courtesy of Auralex Acoustics, Inc.)

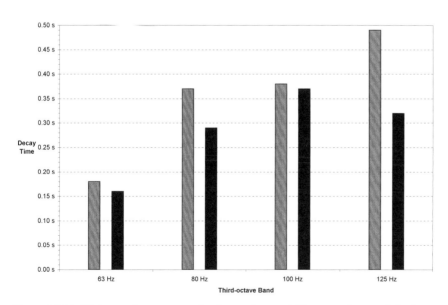

Figure 15.11: This graph compares the decay time at 1/3-octave intervals before and after treatment. (Courtesy of Auralex Acoustics, Inc.)

While the SpaceCouplers certainly worked well for this application, similar results could have been obtained by fitting absorptive panels into the drop ceiling, then covering the panels with as much absorption as possible to improve low-frequency performance.

Reflections

Reflection treatment for this space was made much easier by the distance of the listening position from the side walls. All that was necessary was to apply a few 2-foot by 4-foot absorptive panels to the rear wall, to cure reflections back to the listening position, and to treat the wall behind the monitors with four 2-foot by 4-foot absorptive panels.

Figure 15.12
Spikes screwed to the wall were used to mount glass fiber panels. (Photo by David Stewart.)

To mount the panels behind the monitors, a row of "impalers" was screwed to the wall. The rigid glass fiber panels simply push down onto the spikes—simple, and it works. The same thing could be accomplished with a row of nails or screws sticking out of the wall—be sure not to let the screws or nails stick out so much they pop through the other side of the panel!

If you decide to use acoustic foam instead of glass fiber panels, you have several options for mounting it. You can glue the foam straight to the wall. (Be sure to use approved glue because some types can eat through the foam.) This works great, but is a pretty permanent solution—getting the glue off the wall later is a chore! You could also mount the foam to a thin backing board, then mount the board to the wall; either hang it like a picture or screw through the board into the wall.

Figure 15.13
A laser level (upper left) was used to ensure a straight line when mounting the panels. (Photo by David Stewart.)

Figure 15.14
The same method was used to mount the panels to the rear wall of the space. Not shown is a third panel that hangs on the front of the door. This panel was mounted to a light, thin board, then hung from a thin hook over the door. (Photo by David Stewart.)

For increased low-frequency performance, you could glue the foam to lattice, then mount the lattice to the wall using spacers to achieve an air space behind the foam. (See Chapter 17, "Studio Gallery: Bonus Room," for more on this technique.)

The graph in Figure 15.15 shows the frequency response of the room from 2,000 Hz to 5,000 Hz, before and after treatment with just six rigid glass fiber panels. Note the effect on the huge dip near 3,000 Hz.

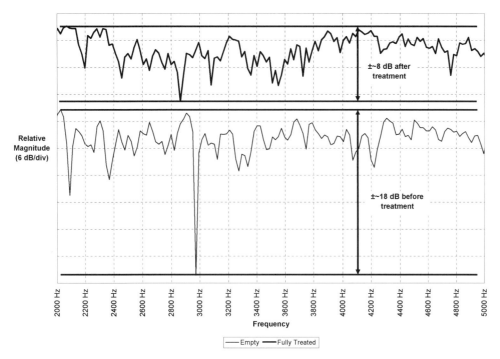

Figure 15.15: The high frequency response of the room before and after treatment. The range of levels has improved from 36 dB (±18 dB) to 16 dB (±8 dB). (Courtesy of Auralex Acoustics, Inc.)

This is the extent of the treatment that we applied to this room. After having built several studios, I prefer to be as minimal as possible with treatments—while, of course, still treating the room adequately for great response and sound. It's very easy to over-treat a room, especially with mid- and high-frequency absorption, and suck the life out of the space.

After doing extensive critical listening in the studio, I couldn't be happier with the results. The "sweet spot" is quite extended, both to the sides and front-to-back. The evenness of the low frequencies is truly amazing—I'm able to hear the pitch and timbre of bass instruments much

155

better, and, in fact, I'm hearing low notes that I've never heard in other spaces without using a subwoofer for extra reinforcement.

The mids and highs are smooth and even with one exception: It quickly became clear that there was a reflection and accompanying cancellation coming off the Digidesign Control 24 control surface/console. If you think you may have this problem, you can double-check with a mirror in the same way as we used a mirror to find the first reflection points for the walls. Lay the mirror on the surface of the console; if you can see the tweeters reflected in the mirror, you have a problem. (To be thorough, you can use the mirror in the same fashion to check any surfaces that are around the primary listening position—racks, tables, desks, computer monitors, and so on.)

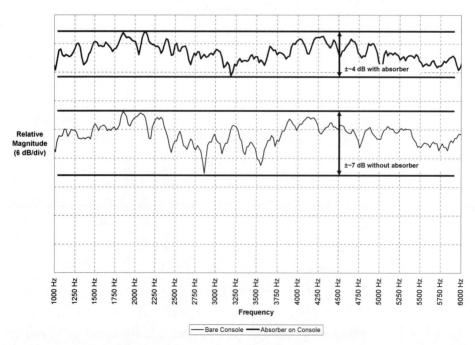

Figure 15.16: Think reflections off a console or desk between you and the monitors don't make a difference? (Courtesy of Auralex Acoustics, Inc.)

Reflections off a console or desk between you and the monitors make a definite difference. The graph in Figure 15.16 shows response with the console (bottom) and with the console covered with absorption (top). Adding the absorption reduced the range from peak to dip by 6 dB, from 14 dB (±7 dB) to 8 dB (±4 dB) in the high frequencies, and significantly smoothed the response.

There are several possible solutions to reflections from the console:

▶ Move the console forward or back slightly to move the reflection point.

▶ Angle the console or control surface up or down to redirect the reflection.

▶ Place an absorber on the console when you are doing critical listening.

▶ Get rid of the console or control surface, and work entirely in the computer. (Not a great one, but it *is* an option.)

Figure 15.17 shows the finished space with the minimal treatments that were applied: Five absorbers/diffusors in the ceiling, four panels on the front wall, and two (or three with the optional one on the door) panels on the back wall.

Figure 15.17
Who says you have to get
carried away with acoustic
treatment? (Photo by David
Stewart.)

Figure 15.18 provides another look at the finished space.

Figure 15.18
All that remains is to decide
on the final furniture that will
be used to house the gear, and
the studio will be complete!
(Photo by David Stewart.)

CHAPTER 16

Studio Gallery: Bedroom

We have a unique opportunity in this chapter. We're treating a simple bedroom space….

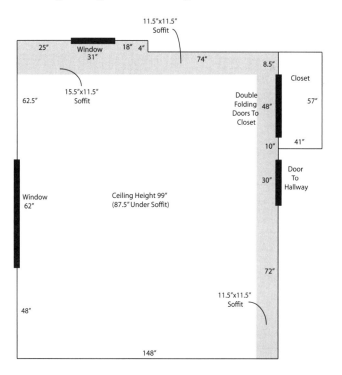

So what's the big opportunity? Looks like a regular corner bedroom, right? The sort of space you'd find in just about any home. Here's the big deal: I solicited studio designs from five different sources—two top-name studio designers, including Russ Berger of Russ Berger Design Group, whom we met earlier in this book, and John Storyk of Walters-Storyk Design Group, who has designed countless studios, home theaters, and other spaces—check out his portfolio at www.wsdg.com. The other designs came from acoustic treatment companies: RealTraps, Auralex Acoustics, and Primacoustic. Berger and Storyk specified various treatments, while the three acoustics companies specified products from their respective catalogs. All of the designers created plans based primarily around stereo monitoring, but with the option to add surround (5.1) monitoring if desired.

The room is roughly 14 feet long by 12 feet wide and slightly over 8 feet high. The walls and ceiling are gypsum wallboard. The carpet has been removed from the floor, revealing the bare concrete underneath. There is a largish closet in one corner, with double metal folding doors. There is a soffit covering ductwork that runs around the ceiling on two walls. Two windows look out onto a nicely landscaped backyard. With six hard surfaces—including a concrete floor—we're talking one *live* room here. Clap your hands, and the reverberations would ring on for quite some time.

Figure 16.1
This analysis shows the low-
frequency response for the
untreated room. (Courtesy of
Auralex Acoustics, Inc.)

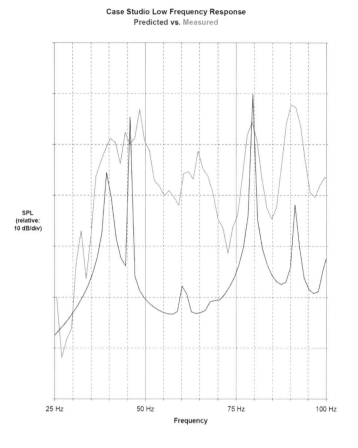

Case Studio Low Frequency Response
Predicted **vs.** Measured

SPL
(relative:
10 dB/div)

25 Hz   50 Hz   75 Hz   100 Hz
Frequency

Primacoustic

Peter Janis of Primacoustic focused on controlling reflections, and low-frequency problems in the 77, 90, and
137 Hz range (calculated based on the room's dimensions). He recommends facing the listener toward the
blank wall, with the speakers firing down the longest
dimension in the room.

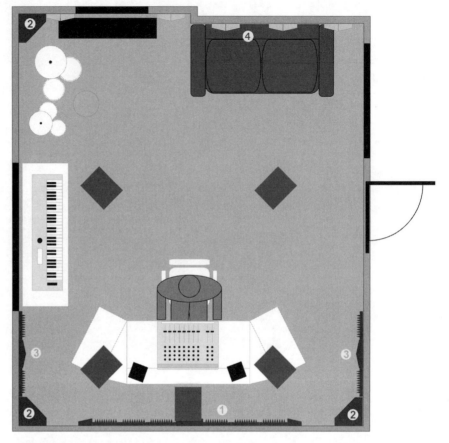

Figure 16.2: The Primacoustic design utilizes a variety of foam treatments to create a live-end/dead-end studio. (Courtesy of Primacoustic.)

Janis specified five treatments (indicated with circled numbers on the diagram).

1. Europa 83. This is a 36-inch by 96-inch foam wedge design with solid foam blocks that can be arranged by the user to create a unique look. The Europa is intended to reduce rear reflections from the monitors.

2. Australis. Six of these foam bass traps are employed to shape low-frequency response, as well as to provide

mid- and high-frequency absorption. These corner traps are 12 inches deep, made from solid foam.

3. Orientique. These 36-inch by 36-inch foam "washboard" panels mount to the side walls and are intended to reduce flutter echo, standing waves, and first-reflection problems.

4. Scandia. "Scatter blocks" are mounted to the rear wall to reduce front-to-back reflections. These foam panels provide primarily absorption, but they also provide what Primacoustic calls "soft diffusion" to help scatter sound energy.

5. The ceiling above the listening position is treated with a Cloud-9 ceiling kit (not shown in the diagram), which creates an absorptive cloud. The result is a reflection-free zone, and a live feel in the rear of the room, emulating the classic live-end, dead-end studio design.

Janis recommends furnishing the room with a soft sofa, which will help treat room modes and provide high-frequency absorption. A low bookcase below the window will provide extra diffusion in the rear of the room. If the room is too live, Janis recommends treating the front side of the soffit with absorption.

RealTraps

Ethan Winer from RealTraps recommends orienting the studio so the monitors fire down the length of the room. He specifies the listening position as 38% of the distance into the room as best for avoiding sitting in a mode's peak or a dip. His philosophy is to move the listening position a few inches to either side to avoid sitting exactly in a left-right modal dip.

Winer's design uses three of his company's products to treat the room. He says that these treatments can be installed with minimal damage to the surfaces of the room.

Figure 16.3
The RealTraps design uses extensive broadband absorption to control low-frequency problems. (Courtesy of RealTraps.)

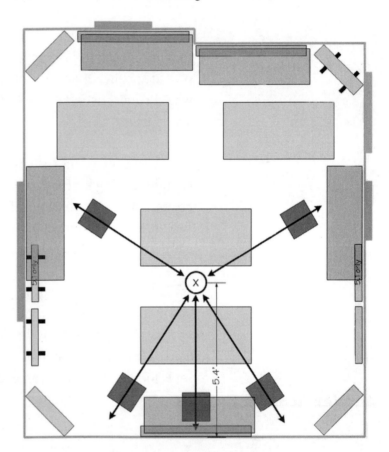

1. Four MondoTraps are used as broadband absorbers in the wall-to-wall corners of the room. Three of these are mounted to the walls, while the fourth, which is in the corner with the closet, is mounted to a stand.

2. Five MiniTraps are mounted at 45 degrees in the wall-to-ceiling corners to provide additional broadband absorption.

3. Two additional MiniTraps are mounted on the rear wall to absorb reflections, since the back wall is less than 10 feet behind the listening position.

4. One additional MiniTrap is mounted horizontally on the front wall behind the monitors.

5. For first reflection control, Winer specified six MicroTraps, which are lightweight and absorb primarily midrange and high frequencies. Two MicroTraps are mounted to each side wall, and two are mounted to the ceiling above the listening position. The MicroTraps for the side of the room with the window are mounted to stands.

6. If the rear of the room will be used for recording vocals or instruments, two more MicroTraps can optionally be installed to the ceiling above that part of the room to help cut down on reflection problems. (The diagram shows these optional MicroTraps in place.)

Auralex Acoustics

The Auralex design focuses on controlling reverberant decay in the room. Jeff Szymanski of Auralex measured the decay time in the room at 0.45 seconds, more than double the decay time most control rooms try to achieve. Using absorption, Szymanski's plan will knock the decay down to around 0.35 seconds—longer than desired for a control room, but the liveness will allow the room to be satisfactory for tracking as well.

Figure 16.4
The focus of the Auralex
Acoustics design is control-
ling reverberation decay.
(Courtesy of Auralex
Acoustics, Inc.)

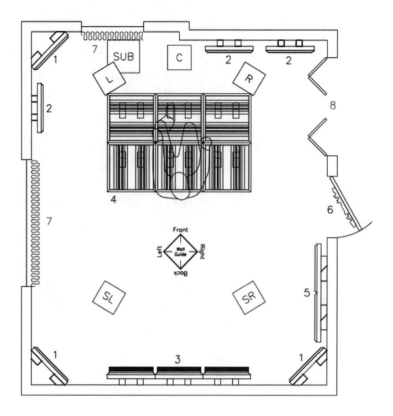

The Auralex plan combines absorption and diffusion. (The numbers in the following list match the numbers in the diagram.) Note that the studio is oriented with the monitors firing down the length of the room, with the listener facing toward the wall with the window.

1. TruTraps absorption panels are mounted at 45 degrees across the room corners to provide broadband absorption.

2. Two TruTraps are mounted to the front wall, and a third is mounted to the left wall to help reduce reflections.

3. Three more TruTraps are mounted to the rear wall to control back-to-front reflections. But in addition to the absorption, Q'Fusors are mounted to the face of the TruTraps to provide diffusion off the back wall.

4. The ceiling above the listening position is covered with three TruTrap panels. If more diffusion is desired, Q'Fusors could be affixed to these panels.

5. One TruTrap panel is mounted horizontally to the rear right wall.

6. The door to the room is treated with two Q'Fusor diffusors to break up reflections.

7. Szymanski recommends covering the windows with heavy curtains. The curtains should be allowed to gather and fold for maximum acoustic effectiveness.

The closet could optionally be filled with insulation, clothing, or other absorptive materials to provide even more broadband absorption.

Walters-Storyk Design Group

John Storyk takes into account the complete room when creating a design. This includes how the gear will be set up and how the room will be oriented. Storyk has elected to face the studio toward the large window, allowing an unobstructed view of the backyard and effectively removing the window as a treatment problem.

Figure 16.5
The Walters-Storyk Design
Group studio plan combines
broadband diffusion with
several types of absorption.
(Courtesy of Walters-Storyk
Design Group.)

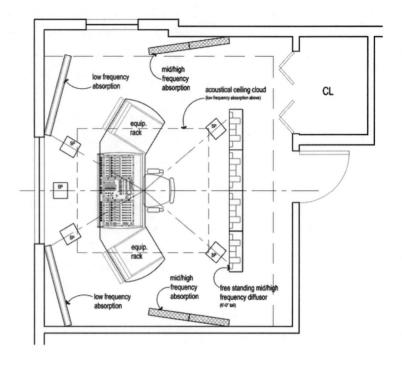

Before creating the design, John Storyk analyzed the room using specialized software to figure out where the problematic room modes will fall. His plan specified that the front corners of the room be treated with low-frequency absorbers.

Storyk uses ray tracing or reflection control analysis to map out reflections that will cause problems in a room. He attacked the reflection problems with a dual approach: midrange and high-frequency absorption on the side walls to address the first reflections, and a free-standing broadband diffusor behind the listening position. The placement of the diffusor will break up rear-to-front reflections and will also serve another purpose: creating an area behind the diffusor that can be used for tracking vocals or instruments. Storyk says the diffusor will extend the width of the listening position sweet spot and improve stereo imaging.

A custom-built cloud hanging from the ceiling above the listening position would provide midrange and high-frequency absorption. Low-frequency absorbers could be placed above the cloud for additional control over room modes.

Storyk recommends placing all speakers on stands, rather than on a console "bridge" or on the desk holding the console or control surface; this will help reduce reflection problems off the console. He also recommends trying the room without a rug on the floor; if the room is too live, a rug could be added to reduce floor reflections as necessary.

Russ Berger Design Group

The Russ Berger design orients the listener toward the blank wall, with the monitors firing the length of the room. The listening position is placed six feet, six inches from the front wall, with the monitors at least two feet from the front wall to reduce low-frequency build-up.

RBDG's analysis of the room predicts a large hole centered around 160 Hz. The plan calls for heavy absorption in the front corners of the room—4- to 6-inch-thick glass fiber absorption from floor to ceiling, angled to three feet from the corner. This will provide broadband absorption, as well as help to redirect reflections.

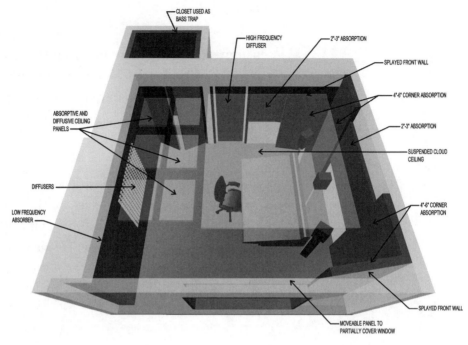

CLOSET USED AS
BASS TRAP

HIGH FREQUENCY
DIFFUSER

2"-3" ABSORPTION

SPLAYED FRONT WALL

4"-6" CORNER ABSORPTION

2"-3" ABSORPTION

SUSPENDED CLOUD
CEILING

ABSORPTIVE AND
DIFFUSIVE CEILING
PANELS

DIFFUSERS

LOW FREQUENCY
ABSORBER

4"-6" CORNER
ABSORPTION

SPLAYED FRONT WALL

MOVEABLE PANEL TO
PARTIALLY COVER WINDOW

Figure 16.6: The Russ Berger Design Group plan covers one of the room's windows and treats the other with absorption on a movable panel. (Courtesy of Russ Berger Design Group.)

Berger recommends covering the rear wall with diffusion in the center and thick absorption for the remainder of the wall. He suggests plugging the window and continuing the thick absorption to the corner. The other window is treated with a movable panel; the treatment can be hinged, sliding, or mounted to a stand.

An absorptive cloud is hung two to four inches below the ceiling, providing first reflection control and broadband absorption. This cloud covers the front two-thirds of the room. The remaining ceiling is treated with absorption and diffusion, which will help even out the response in the rear of the room.

The front and side walls are treated with absorption from three feet from the floor to seven feet from the floor to control reflections. Diffusion is mounted to the door.

Berger recommends using the closet to house computers and noisy equipment. The closet should be lined with absorption. For even better performance, replace the closet doors with wooden frames surrounding absorptive panels. This turns the closet into a large bass trap.

Yet Another Take

Even in such illustrious, knowledgeable, and experienced company, far be it from me to refrain from getting my two cents in! Here's a design for the room using primarily absorptive panels.

We begin by treating the corners of the room with absorptive panels floor to ceiling to create broadband absorbers. We'll steal a trick from the RealTraps design and mount the absorber in the rear right corner (the one with the closet) on a stand.

The front wall and side walls are treated with 2-foot by 4-foot absorptive panels. One panel is mounted to a stand and placed in front of the window. The ceiling is also treated with 2-foot by 4-foot panels.

Figure 16.7
Absorptive panels and book-
cases used for diffusion are
the main features of this
design for our bedroom.

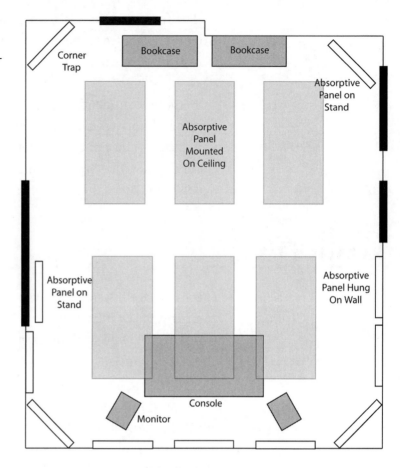

Two large bookcases are placed against the rear wall for diffusion. One covers most of the rear window; the two bookcases are aligned to make the back wall even, removing some of the effects of the jog in the rear wall.

The closet can be used for storage or it can be treated with absorption and used as a "machine closet" for noisy computers and other equipment. For best results, the doors should be replaced with something heavier than the current light metal units, or at least the metal doors should be treated inside and out with absorption to prevent rattling or the doors resonating.

CHAPTER 17

Visual Representations of Studio Gallery: Bonus Room

The next studio in our gallery is a "bonus room" that became a studio for me in Nashville—the room is a large space above a two-stall garage. The space connects to the rest of the house with a staircase; there's a full bathroom at the back of the room. The studio is all in one room; the area behind the "control room" area is used for tracking.

The "front" of the room has a large window. Because the room is above the garage, there are 5-foot "knee" walls, connecting to an angled part of the ceiling (which follows the roof line of the garage), which connects to a flat portion of the ceiling. The floor is hardwood; the walls and ceiling are gypsum wallboard. The room is 23 feet long (26 feet with alcove) by 19 feet wide by 9 feet high at the highest point of the ceiling.

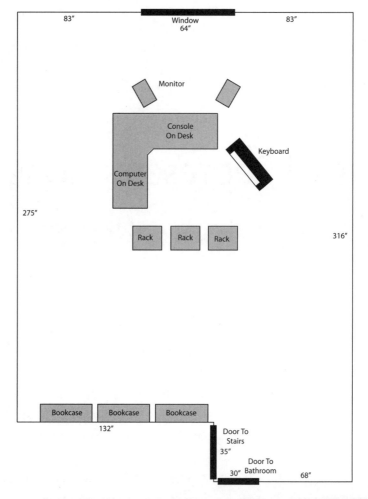

Figure 17.1
The bonus room is a large
space with an alcove in the
rear and an adjoining full
bathroom.

Figure 17.2
Looking toward the back of
the room before any gear has
been unpacked or installed.
This shot shows the alcove
and the entrance to the full
bath. Note the "knee" walls
and angled ceiling sections.

Figure 17.3
Looking toward the front of
the room, with the large win-
dow, and another view of the
angled ceiling walls.

The Pro Design

John Storyk of the Walters-Storyk Design Group (whom we met in the last chapter) agreed to create a plan for acoustically treating this space. The room is symmetrical when facing toward the window, so the studio was oriented with the listener looking at the window, with the monitor speakers firing the long way in the room. This put the asymmetrical "alcove" part of the room behind the listener. While the effects of the alcove were audible, Storyk had a solution for solving this problem— building a short wall extension. The plan for the room involved extensive low-frequency trapping using membrane bass traps, and a reflection-free zone created around the listening position.

As Figure 17.4 shows, John Storyk's floor plan for the studio incorporates side wall absorption, diffusion centered on the rear wall mounted to an extension that covers part of the alcove, and a bench on the front wall that conceals bass trapping on the sides and contains storage space in the center. There is also additional storage on the two side walls in the back of the room.

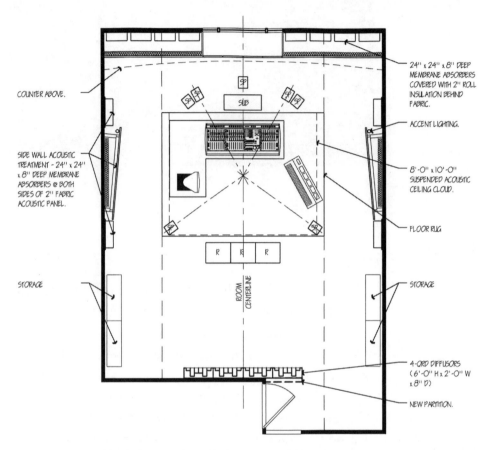

COUNTER ABOVE.

24" x 24" x 8" DEEP MEMBRANE ABSORBERS COVERED WITH 2" ROLL INSULATION BEHIND FABRIC.

ACCENT LIGHTING.

SIDE WALL ACOUSTIC TREATMENT - 24" x 24" x 8" DEEP MEMBRANE ABSORBERS @ BOTH SIDES OF 2" FABRIC ACOUSTIC PANEL.

8'-0" x 10'-0" SUSPENDED ACOUSTIC CEILING CLOUD.

FLOOR RUG

SUB

STORAGE

ROOM CENTERLINE

STORAGE

4-ORD DIFFUSORS (6'-0" H x 2'-0" W x 8" D)

NEW PARTITION.

Figure 17.4: Storyk's plan uses side wall absorption, diffusion centered on the rear wall mounted to an extension, and a bench that conceals bass trapping. (Courtesy of Walters-Storyk Design Group.)

As you can see in Figure 17.5, looking up toward the ceiling, there is absorption mounted to the angled walls and a large absorptive cloud suspended over the listening position. The cloud conceals bass traps that have been mounted to the ceiling. Track lighting is mounted to the cloud as well.

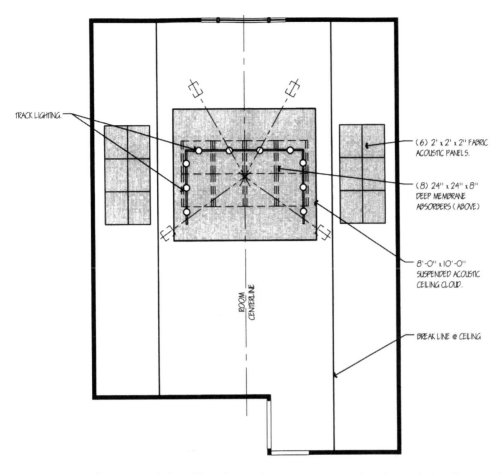

TRACK LIGHTING.

(6) 2' x 2' x 2" FABRIC
ACOUSTIC PANELS.

(8) 24" x 24" x 8"
DEEP MEMBRANE
ABSORBERS (ABOVE)

8'-0" x 10'-0"
SUSPENDED ACOUSTIC
CEILING CLOUD.

BREAK LINE @ CEILING

ROOM
CENTERLINE

Figure 17.5: Looking toward the ceiling shows absorption mounted to the angled walls, as well as a large absorptive cloud. (Courtesy of Walters-Storyk Design Group.)

Figure 17.6 shows the room's side walls; you can see the detail of how bass traps are mounted above the ceiling cloud and inside the bench running across the front of the room.

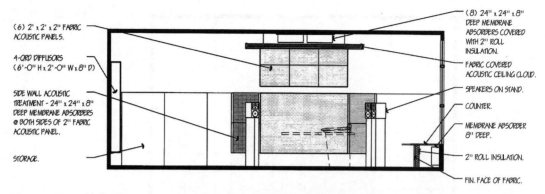

Figure 17.6: The bass traps are mounted above the ceiling cloud and inside the bench at the front of the room. (Courtesy of Walters-Storyk Design Group.)

Views of the front and rear elevations of the room, as in Figure 17.7, show the diffusion mounted to the rear wall, extending past the end of the existing wall. The front view shows detail of bass traps on the ceiling and front wall, and the storage cabinets built into the center of the front wall bench between the bass traps.

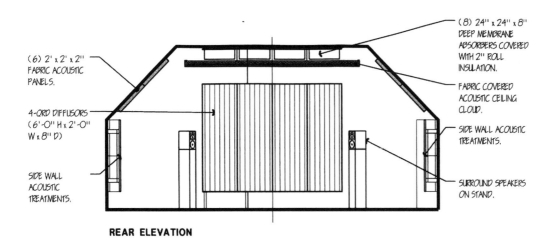

(6) 2' x 2' x 2"
FABRIC ACOUSTIC
PANELS.

4-ORD DIFFUSORS
(6'-O" H x 2'-O"
W x 8" D)

SIDE WALL
ACOUSTIC
TREATMENTS.

(8) 24" x 24" x 8"
DEEP MEMBRANE
ABSORBERS COVERED
WITH 2" ROLL
INSULATION.

FABRIC COVERED
ACOUSTIC CEILING
CLOUD.

SIDE WALL ACOUSTIC
TREATMENTS.

SURROUND SPEAKERS
ON STAND.

REAR ELEVATION

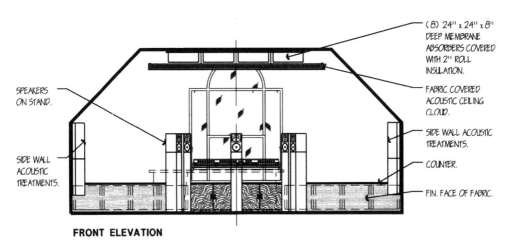

SPEAKERS
ON STAND.

SIDE WALL
ACOUSTIC
TREATMENTS.

(8) 24" x 24" x 8"
DEEP MEMBRANE
ABSORBERS COVERED
WITH 2" ROLL
INSULATION.

FABRIC COVERED
ACOUSTIC CEILING
CLOUD.

SIDE WALL ACOUSTIC
TREATMENTS.

COUNTER.

FIN. FACE OF FABRIC.

FRONT ELEVATION

*Figure 17.7: The diffusion mounted to the rear wall extends past the end of the existing wall.
(Courtesy of Walters-Storyk Design Group.)*

Treatments

There are a variety of treatments used in John Storyk's plan:

1. A bench, or shelf, is built across the front of the room. Membrane-type bass traps are placed under the bench, along the bottom of the wall, to help control room modes based on the length dimension. (Storyk recommends using RPG MODEX units.) The front of the bench is covered with fabric to conceal the traps. In the center of the room, the area under the bench contains built-in storage.

2. Membrane bass traps are mounted to the vertical side walls in front of and behind the listening position. Glass fiber panels are mounted at an angle between these traps; the angle spaces the panels away from the wall, improving low-frequency response. Storyk suggests mounting lighting behind the panels to create a backlit effect.

3. The angled ceiling is treated with six 2-foot by 2-foot absorptive panels.

4. A custom-built absorptive cloud, 8 feet by 10 feet, is hung from the ceiling. Track lighting is mounted to the underside of the cloud. (The room's light fixture/ceiling fan is removed.)

5. More membrane bass traps are mounted to the ceiling above the cloud. Glass fiber insulation is also rolled out on top of the cloud.

6. A large Quadratic Residue Diffusor is mounted to the
   back wall. Storyk suggests that the diffusor be large
   enough to extend beyond the existing back wall, so
   that the alcove in the rear of the room is partially
   covered and the rear reflections are evened out.
   (Storyk recommends the RPG QRD diffusors for this
   application.)

Figure 17.8
The final layout of the room,
using substitute acoustical
treatments.

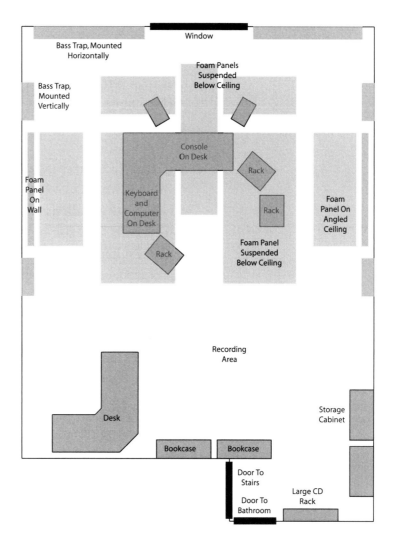

The Real World

Storyk estimates the cost of treating the room using this plan at around $10,000, assuming you did all the work yourself. Not a ridiculous price, but still way out of the range of my checkbook. I elected to follow Storyk's plan, but to substitute less expensive treatments, as shown in Figure 17.8.

1. I substituted 4-inch-thick acoustic foam for the glass fiber panels on the side walls and the angled ceilings. The foam was mounted to lattice and spaced four inches from the wall to improve low-frequency performance. I used three 2-foot by 4-foot foam pieces glued to the lattice to create 4-foot by 6-foot panels.

As Figure 17.9 shows, regular plastic garden lattice was reinforced with 2×2 wood, then mounted to the vertical and angled walls as well as the ceiling, using hooks and eyebolts. The combination of the wood frame and hooks resulted in the lattice being spaced four inches off the surface, improving low-frequency absorption.

Figure 17.9
This photo shows the lattice fitted in place as a test; the foam was glued to the lattice before the final mounting of the panel to the wall or ceiling.

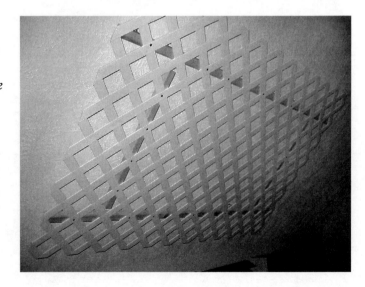

Figure 17.10
A finished foam panel mounted to the wall beside a 2-foot by 4-foot wooden panel bass trap. The lattice above will be taken down, covered with foam, then re-hooked on the wall.

2. The ceiling had several HVAC vents that I didn't want to cover. So I broke the cloud up into pieces and mounted them with gaps to allow for air to flow from the vents. The panels on the ceiling were built the same way as the panels on the walls, from 2-foot by 4-foot foam pieces. Track mounting was mounted to the front of the large ceiling panels. (The ceiling fan/lighting fixture was removed.)

3. RealTraps wooden panel-type bass traps were used for low-frequency control. Four 2-foot by 4-foot traps were mounted vertically on the side walls. Two 4-foot by 6-foot traps were mounted horizontally along the bottom of the front wall. (Note: RealTraps no longer makes these traps; the company now focuses on broadband absorption.)

In Figure 17.11, the room is nearing completion. Most of the foam panels have been installed. (Note

183

the separate panels on the ceiling instead of one big cloud; this allows for the vents.) The front wall features horizontally mounted 2-foot by 6-foot wooden bass traps, while the side walls feature 2-foot by 4-foot wooden bass traps mounted vertically. The traps have angled faces, which helps to redirect reflections. The ceiling fan/light fixture hasn't been removed yet, nor has the track lighting been installed.

Figure 17.11
The room is nearing completion.

4. Large bookcases were placed at the center of the rear wall, with one extending over the opening into the alcove.

The furniture and gear in the room were moved around to create a more accessible "control room," a larger recording space, and to make room for a small office area. A large rug was positioned under the control room area; the floor of the recording area was left bare hardwood. Two storage cabinets were placed on the side walls, at the back of the room, and a large CD rack went against the back wall of the alcove.

Figure 17.12 shows the finished room, with all panels installed and track lighting mounted to the ceiling panels. The gear has been rearranged from the original plan, and a rug has been placed under the "control room" area of the room.

Figure 17.12
The gear has been rearranged from the original plan for the finished room.

The result was a very fine-sounding room. The reflection-free zone allowed for excellent imaging, and with the size of the room and the bass trapping, the low end was solid and even almost anywhere you listened.

CHAPTER 18

Studio Gallery: Recording Booth

Next up in our studio gallery is a recording booth. Generally booths are quite small—large enough for a single vocalist, or perhaps an acoustic guitarist, or maybe a horn player, or a guitar amp. Because booths tend to be small—in many cases even a closet is spacious enough to record a vocalist or a guitar amp—the sound of the room is a big problem. Usually a very small untreated space has a "boxy" sound, with an odd ring, powerful flutter echoes, and awful low-frequency response.

Many choose to address the boxiness and reflection problems with lots of mid- and high-frequency absorption. This results in a completely dead room. And because the highs and mids are so dead, the low frequencies become a real problem. For this reason, broadband absorption is a must, though many people skip this important step.

The advantage to making the room totally dead is that it imparts no character to your recordings. You can add whatever ambience you want using electronic reverberation and delays. The disadvantage is that the room is totally dead, which may make it an uncomfortable area in which to perform.

I don't believe that a very small space such as a recording booth has to be completely dead. I prefer to treat it like any other room: Address the low-frequency problems using broadband absorption, then treat flutter echo and reflection problems with mid- and high-frequency absorption. Since there isn't a single, predictable point source as there is with a speaker in a control room, we do have to allow for different sound sources being placed in various locations inside the booth: guitar amps near the floor, seated acoustic guitarists, standing vocalists, and so on. For this reason, all the surfaces of the room receive some treatment to cut down on potential reflections.

The booth we're looking at is in the same basement as our room in Chapter 15. It's 9-1/2 feet long by roughly 6-1/2 feet wide and nearly 7-1/2 feet high. One corner of the room is cut off, resulting in an angled surface where the entry door is located. The walls are gypsum wallboard, there is a drop ceiling, and the floor is carpeted. Clapping your hands in the booth results in the characteristic fast flutters and ring of a small, hard room.

Figure 18.1
The booth is large enough for one person to work in very comfortably; two people will also be able to work in there nicely. It can accommodate more artists than this, but things will get cozy!

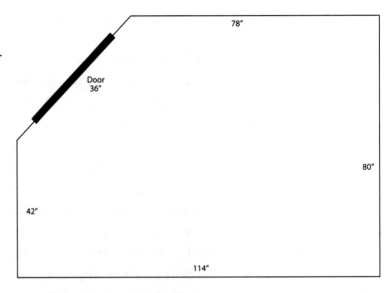

Figure 18.2
The booth has gypsum wallboard walls, carpet on the floor, and a drop ceiling. (Photo by David Stewart.)

As a benchmark, frequency sweeps were recorded and analyzed in the booth in three different positions—where the mic would be placed when recording a guitar amp, a seated acoustic guitarist, and a standing vocalist. As we saw in Chapter 15, moving the microphone to different positions in the room can dramatically change the low-frequency response.

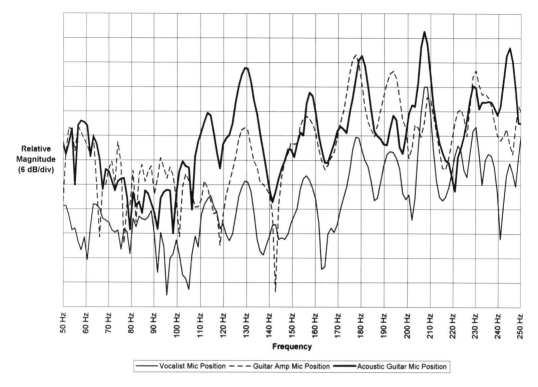

Figure 18.3: Frequency response at three microphone positions in the room. (Courtesy of Auralex Acoustics, Inc.)

The graph in Figure 18.4 shows the analyzed frequency response for the booth with the microphone in the acoustic guitar position, with the calculated room modes superimposed (arrows). For reference, the musical notes are overlaid on the graph (at the top of the graph), with open guitar string pitches marked. Note the uneven room response at each pitch. This may make some notes sound boomy and others seem dead.

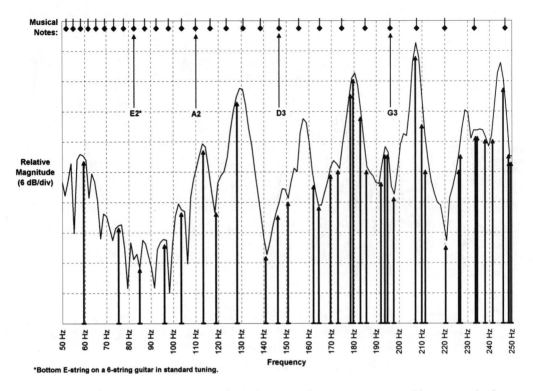

Figure 18.4: Uneven room response at each pitch may make some notes sound boomy and others seem dead. (Courtesy of Auralex Acoustics, Inc.)

Treatment

We'll take a straight-ahead approach to treating the booth, utilizing the same concepts we've used in earlier chapters. We won't be going for a completely dead space; rather, we'll be creating a neutral space frequency response-wise, with a bit of life left so that the room will be pleasant for musicians to perform in.

The booth will be treated primarily with 2-inch-thick 2-foot by 4-foot rigid glass-fiber panels. The corners will be treated with panels at 45 degrees to create broadband absorbers. Panels will also be placed on the walls for mid- and high-frequency absorption. One-inch-thick 2-foot by 2-foot panels will be inserted in the drop ceiling grid. (See Figure 18.5.)

Figure 18.5
The booth will be treated primarily with 2-inch-thick 2-foot by 4-foot rigid glass-fiber panels.

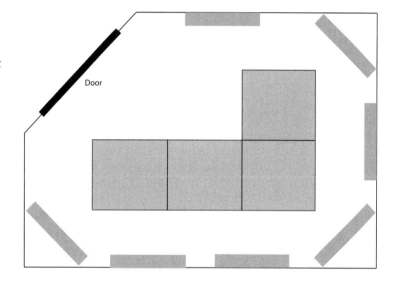

Door

Four treatments will be applied to the booth.

1. Three 2-inch-thick 2-foot by 4-foot absorptive panels will be mounted at 45 degrees across the room corners for broadband absorption. For even more absorption, the corners could be covered from floor to ceiling.

Figure 18.6
Spikes were screwed to the walls to mount the absorptive panels. (Photo by David Stewart.)

Figure 18.7
Absorptive panels were mounted
across the corners to create broad-
band absorbers. (Photo by David
Stewart.)

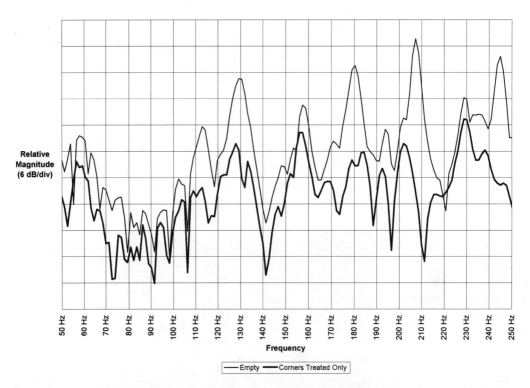

Figure 18.8: Applying the three corner absorbers made a significant improvement in the low-frequency response in the room. (Courtesy of Auralex Acoustics, Inc.)

As shown in Figure 18.9, the booth's frequency response was measured as if the microphone were recording an acoustic guitar.

Figure 18.9
The top speaker was the only one that was active; the others were serving as a "stand" for the top speaker. (Photo by David Stewart.)

2. Four 2-inch-thick 2-foot by 4-foot absorptive panels will be mounted on the walls for mid- and high-frequency reflection control.

3. Four 1-inch-thick 2-foot by 2-foot panels will be used in the drop ceiling. Additional absorption will be placed above the panels to increase low-frequency effectiveness.

Figure 18.10
Two-inch-thick panels were
applied to the walls for
mid- and high-frequency
absorption. One-inch-thick
panels were dropped into
the ceiling grid, with extra
absorption on top to increase
low-frequency absorption.
(Photo by David Stewart.)

4. Because I had some extra Auralex LENRD (*Low End Node Reduction Device*) foam corner traps available, I placed three at the wall-to-wall-to-floor junctions, partially behind the corner panels.

Figure 18.11
Auralex LENRD foam corner
traps were added to the floor
corners for extra absorption.
(Photo by David Stewart.)

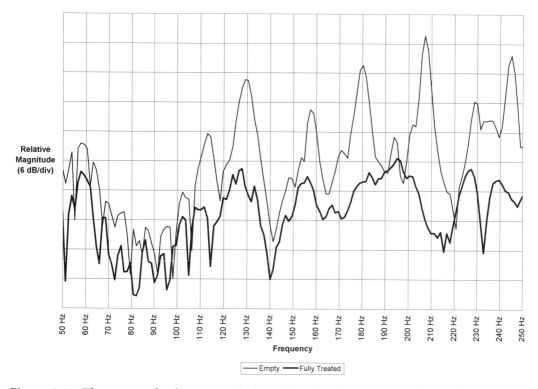

Figure 18.12: The response for the room with the wall and ceiling treatments installed shows even more smoothing in the low frequencies. (Courtesy of Auralex Acoustics, Inc.)

Don't Stop Now

While the frequency response showed excellent improvement after applying the four treatments listed here, on listening to the booth, there was still a bit of boxiness to the sound in the midrange frequencies.

To solve this problem, five additional LENRDs (that was all I had available—use what you have) were stacked and placed in the room, about a foot out from the nearest wall.

Figure 18.13
Additional LENRD absorbers
were placed to reduce boxi-
ness in the room. (Photo by
David Stewart.)

This serves to show that while frequency response graphs are wonderful tools, the best tools to use for analyzing a room remain the ears on the side of your head. Adding the LENRDs solved the boxiness problem and made the booth sound very even and smooth, but not too dead.

The graph in Figure 18.14 shows the booth's midrange frequency response with corner, wall, and ceiling treatment (fully treated) versus the fully treated room with the additional LENRD absorbers stacked in it.

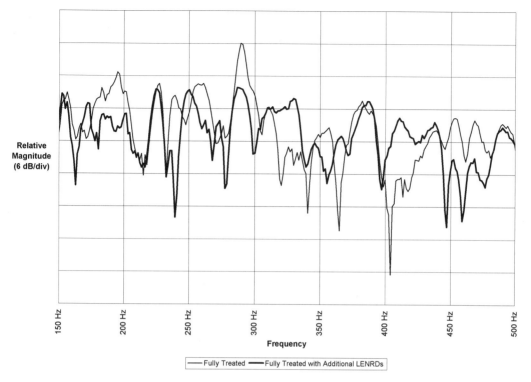

Relative Magnitude (6 dB/div)

Frequency

150 Hz   200 Hz   250 Hz   300 Hz   350 Hz   400 Hz   450 Hz   500 Hz

—— Fully Treated   —— Fully Treated with Additional LENRDs

Figure 18.14: Note the smoothing in the 350 to 400 Hz range—this was the probably the source of the boxiness we heard. (Courtesy of Auralex Acoustics, Inc.)

Figure 18.15 shows another view of the midrange frequency response of the "fully treated" booth versus the fully treated room with additional stacks of LENRDs. The range from peak to dip went from 44 dB (±22 dB) to 26 dB (±13 dB). Amazing improvement, given that all we did was stack an additional five pieces of foam in an already good-sounding room!

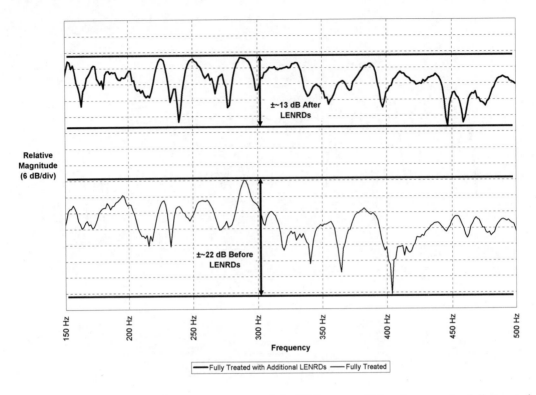

Figure 18.15: The midrange frequency response of the "fully treated" booth versus the fully treated room with additional stacks of LENRDs. (Courtesy of Auralex Acoustics, Inc.)

With the additional LENRD absorbers in the booth, we can do a complete before/after comparison of the room's frequency response.

The graph in Figure 18.16 compares the empty booth at the acoustic guitar position with the fully treated room with the extra LENRDs in place.

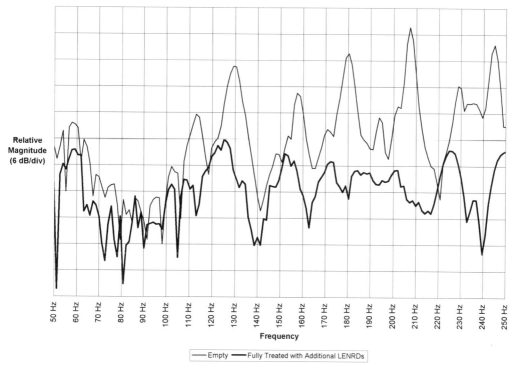

Figure 18.16: Substantial low-frequency improvement! (Courtesy of Auralex Acoustics, Inc.)

Figure 18.17 provides a view of the high frequency response of the empty room versus the fully treated room with LENRDs. The range of levels went from 20 dB (±10 dB) empty to 12 dB (±6 dB) after treatment.

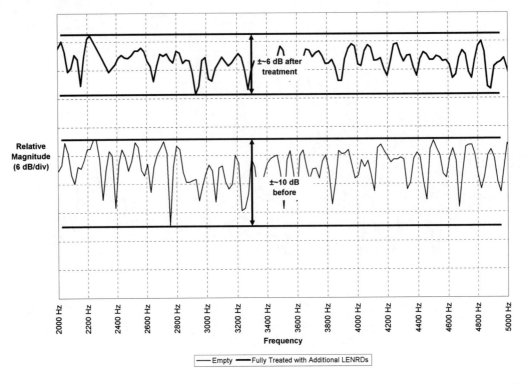

Figure 18.17: The range of peaks and dips is not as broad for high frequencies as for low frequencies. (Courtesy of Auralex Acoustics, Inc.)

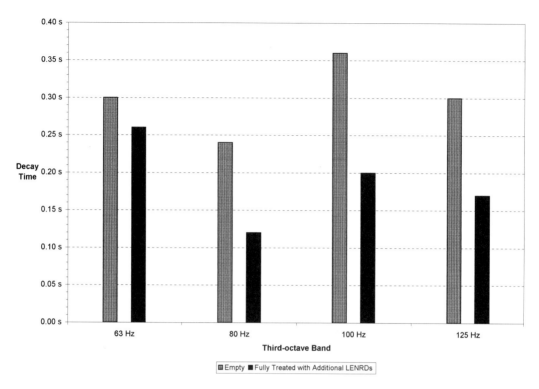

Figure 18.18: There was substantial improvement in the low-frequency reverberant decay in the booth as well. This is especially important for achieving clarity on any "transient" sounds that occur in the space. (Courtesy of Auralex Acoustics, Inc.)

Another way to look at the effects of reflections and low-frequency problems in the room is to consider the "coloration" effects of long decay times.

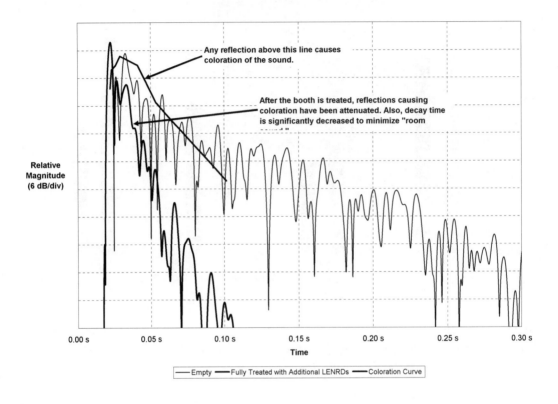

Figure 18.19: This graph shows the reduction in reverberant decay time after the booth was fully treated, with the additional LENRD absorbers stacked in the room. (Courtesy of Auralex Acoustics, Inc.)

Results

After installing the treatments, the room response evened right out, and the room became a great place to track both instruments and vocalists. The smoothing in the lows and the mids made it especially nice for recording nylon- or steel-string acoustic guitar (which was a primary goal).

While we primarily used rigid glass fiber panels to treat the room, acoustic foam could have been used as well. In fact, before installing the glass fiber panels, I treated the room in similar fashion, using 4-inch-thick 2-foot by 4-foot acoustic foam sheets tacked to the walls and ceiling. The results were remarkably similar.

CHAPTER 19

Studio Gallery: Machine Room

There's no getting around it; most home and project studios are based around computers. And even if computers aren't used for recording audio, there's probably a computer there being used for some purpose, such as MIDI sequencing or e-mail.

The problem is that computers make noise—they have cooling fans and hard drives that whirl, click, and whine. You may also be using external hard drives for recording the actual audio data or for backup. And more hard drives mean more cooling fans and more whirling, clicking, and whining.

It all adds up to noise—noise you don't want to pick up in microphones when you're tracking, and noise you don't want to have to listen through when you're mixing. All this was discussed in Chapter 12, where we realized that placing the computers into a closet or adjacent space can be a big help in controlling the noise problem. If you do place the computer, drives, and other fan-equipped gear in a nearby closet, there's still more you can do to reduce noise levels.

The easiest thing is to simply treat the inside of the closet with absorption. The good news is that fans and hard drives emit primarily mid- and high-frequency noise. We won't have to worry about broadband absorption or bass trapping.

In the studio we treated in Chapter 15, there's a handy storage closet behind the listening position.

Figure 19.1
A handy storage closet—even one with a strange shape— makes for a great "machine room" for containing the noise from computers, hard drives, and other gear.

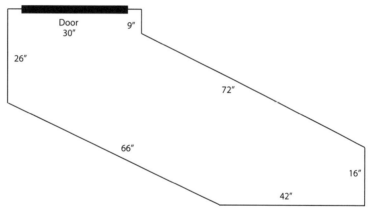

The storage closet is odd-shaped, following the path of the stairway above it. The first half or so of the space is full height, but then the ceiling angles down as the stairs descend. But there's plenty of room for a computer or two, hard drives, audio interfaces with built-in fans, and even a good-sized wall where shelves will be installed to hold recording media, compact discs, software, backup media, or other studio essentials.

The closet has gypsum wallboard walls and ceiling, carpet on the floor, and a heavy solid-wood door. There's enough space under the door to run cables out to the studio (because I'm not wireless, extenders were needed to connect computer monitors, keyboards, and mice), as well as audio connections to the audio interface.

Fortunately, listening tests proved the space under the door to be of little consequence in letting computer noise out of the closet. Another piece of good luck was an opening in the upper part of the closet that let air flow out into the room behind the closet. The room warms up when computers, drives, and interfaces are left running all day, but not to such an extent that there is concern over the equipment overheating. (A word of warning: Be sure to check temperatures thoroughly if you install your computer and other equipment in a closed space—heat is the enemy of all electronic equipment!)

Treatment

This was an easy one. As mentioned a moment ago, the noise generated by computers, hard drives, and other audio equipment falls squarely in the mid- and high-frequency range. And we don't care what our machine room sounds like; all we want is for it to be as quiet as possible.

Given those facts, here's the treatment prescription: Cover all available surfaces with absorption. Make that sucker dead! Just be sure to allow for ventilation. It doesn't have to look good, and it doesn't have to match. Foam, glass fiber, leftover acoustic treatment from other spaces, old clothes, whatever you have that will absorb mids and highs will work fine. Don't forget to treat the ceiling and the inside of the door.

That's it—your machine room is done!

Afterword

There's nothing like recording and mixing music in a great-sounding space. Everything sounds clear, clean, and natural—and it's just so easy. Throw a microphone up on a stand, hit record, and the tracks sound better, with less effort and less struggle. There's no better way to improve your studio than to improve its acoustical performance.

Using the techniques and concepts we've covered in this book, you can turn any space into a much better environment for making music and recording and mixing projects. It's not difficult, and it doesn't have to be expensive or time-consuming.

Just a little planning, a bit of effort, a few materials, and your music and recordings will immediately sound better. Now that's a great investment!

—Mitch Gallagher

Appendix

Resources

MANUFACTURERS AND SOURCES OF ACOUSTICAL MATERIALS

► Acoustics First: www.acousticsfirst.com

► Acoustisoft: www.acoustisoft.com

► Acoustone: www.acoustonegrillecloth.com

► ASC: www.tubetrap.com

► Audio Ease: www.audioease.com

► Auralex Acoustics: www.auralex.com

► Guilford of Maine: www.guilfordofmaine.com

► Illbruck Acoustic: www.illbruck-sonex.com

► Metric Halo Labs: www.mhlabs.com

► NT Instruments: www.nt-instruments.com

▶ Owens Corning: www.owenscorning.com

▶ Primacoustic: www.primacoustic.com

▶ Raxxess: www.raxxess.com

▶ RealTraps: www.realtraps.com

▶ Rose Brand: www.rosebrand.com

▶ RPG Diffusors: www.rpginc.com/proaudio

▶ SIA Software Company, www.siasoft.com

▶ Silent Source: www.silentsource.com

▶ Sound Construction & Supply: www.custom-consoles.com

▶ Studio Panels (Media Specialty Resources): www.msr-inc.com/studiopanel.php

▶ Sweetwater: www.sweetwater.com

▶ TerraSonde: www.terrasonde.com

Studio Designers

▶ Russ Berger Design Group: www.rbdg.com

▶ Walters-Storyk Design Group: www.wsdg.com

Web Resources

- ▶ Acoustical Society of America:
  asa.aip.org

- ▶ Acoustics FAQ:
  www.faqs.org/faqs/physics-faq/acoustics

- ▶ Acoustics.Org:
  www.acoustics.org

- ▶ John Sayers Recording Studio Design Forum:
  www.johnlsayers.com/phpBB2/index.php

- ▶ National Council of Acoustical Consultants:
  www.ncac.com

- ▶ Pro Audio Reference:
  www.rane.com/digi-dic.html

- ▶ SAE Institute:
  www.saecollege.de/reference_material/index.html

- ▶ *Sound On Sound* magazine Acoustic Forum:
  www.soundonsound.com/forum

- ▶ StudioTips and StudioTips Forum:
  www.studiotips.com

Most of the manufacturers and suppliers of acoustic treatment materials also include information and resources on their Web sites.

Glossary

absorber. Acoustical device that reduces the level of sound waves by converting sound energy into heat.

absorption. In acoustics, using "soft" material to reduce the intensity of sound waves. Absorptive materials convert sonic energy into heat in order to reduce sound level.

acoustic coefficient. Rating for the performance of an acoustical material at a particular frequency. Values range from 0 (totally reflective) to 1 (totally absorptive).

acoustic foam. A special type of open cell foam designed to absorb sound waves.

acoustic treatment. Acoustic devices and materials installed in a space to control the behavior of sound. There are three types: absorbers, reflectors, and diffusors.

acoustics. The study of sound or the behavior of sound within an enclosed space.

active monitor. Type of self-contained studio speaker with an amplifier built into the speaker cabinet itself.

AES. Acronym for the Audio Engineering Society.

ambience. 1. Sense of space. 2. The acoustical character of a space.

amplifier. Electronic device used to increase input signals to a higher level.

amplitude. 1. Size or magnitude. 2. The strength or sound pressure level of a signal measured in decibels.

anechoic. 1. Totally dead, literally without echoes. 2. A space that supports no reflection of sound waves. The closest common anechoic situation occurring in nature is the outdoors, but even there, the earth could create some reflection.

anechoic chamber. A specially designed room designed to be totally absorptive at all frequencies. Anechoic chambers are used for testing and measurement of specifications, not for recording or listening to music.

anti-node. A position along a wave at which there is maximum motion.

attack. The beginning portion of a sound.

attack time. The time it takes for a signal to go from silence to maximum level. The character and amount of reverb can be influenced by the attack time of a signal.

attenuate. To reduce the level of a signal.

audio. 1. Sound. 2. Electrical signal representing sound.

axial mode. A mode caused by sound reflecting between two parallel surfaces.

A-weighting. Using a filter to reduce certain frequencies when measuring to obtain results that match better with the frequency response of our ears. Some manufacturers use A-weighted specifications for their gear to disguise poor performance.

background noise. Ambient or environmental noise in a room or space.

bandwidth. Range of frequencies.

bass trap. Acoustic device designed to absorb low-frequency sound waves.

Bel. A unit of measure expressing the amount a signal drops in level over one mile of telephone wire. Named for Alexander Graham Bell.

bleed. Sound waves "leaking" from one space or another, or into a microphone not intended for the sound source that creates them.

broadband. Effective over a wide range of frequencies.

broadband absorber. Acoustic device designed to absorb sound waves across a wide range of frequencies.

cancellation. See *phase cancellation*.

carpet. Poor acoustical absorber best employed on the floor of a room.

close field. See *near field*.

cloud. Acoustical device suspended from the ceiling over the listening position.

coloration. Change in the timbre of a sound or signal.

comb filtering. Series of deep notches and peaks in frequency response, usually due to phase differences between sound waves. Results in significant coloration of the sound.

compression. Area of increased pressure caused by a sound wave. The opposite of a rarefaction.

couch. Marginally effective acoustic absorber well suited to supporting the posterior regions of humans.

C-weighting. Using a flat response, limited bandwidth filter to obtain measurements that correlate better to how our ears hear.

cycles per second. Number of peak/trough cycles in a sound wave that occur in a second. Also known as "frequency" and "Hertz."

DAW. Acronym for Digital Audio Workstation.

dead. All or most reflections absorbed.

decay. The manner in which sound falls to silence.

decay time. See *reverberant decay*.

decibel (dB). 1. One-tenth of a Bel. 2. The ratio between two audio levels. A decibel is an expression of the ratio between an audio signal and a 0 dB reference, and not actually a measurement of audio level. Because of the way in which our ears respond to volume, these ratios are logarithmic in nature. **3.** The smallest volume change the human ear can perceive without a reference to compare against, in isolation.

decoupling. Isolating an object, such as a speaker cabinet, monitor, or even a room's floor or wall, from its surroundings.

diaphragmatic trap. See *membrane trap.*

diffraction. In acoustics, sound waves with long wavelengths bend around objects (diffract) instead of reflecting off them.

diffuse. Scattered or spread out.

diffusion. Breaking a single reflection into many smaller, lower-level reflections scattering in different directions.

diffusor. Also diffuser; "diffusor" is more commonly used in acoustics. An acoustic device that scatters sound waves.

dip. An area where cancellation of sound waves causes a decrease in level at a particular frequency or range of frequencies.

direct field. Speakers or a sound source set up so that the listener primarily hears the direct sound, with few or no reflections. See also *near field*.

direct sound. Sound from a source that arrives at the listener's ears without reflecting off any surfaces.

directional. Moving in a single direction.

dispersion. 1. Scattering or distribution of sound waves as they travel from a sound source, such as a speaker. 2. The angle of coverage a speaker can produce. (There are two such specifications for speakers: vertical and horizontal.)

distortion. Literally, any change in a signal other than making it louder or softer—this would include equalization, compression, and other forms of processing. But in practice, distortion tends to be considered a negative or undesirable chance in a signal's waveform.

driver. Element of a speaker or monitor that creates sound waves.

dry. A sound or signal without reverberation or other processing on it.

dynamic range. The ratio (in decibels) of the loudest to the softest signals a system can handle without distortion.

early reflection. The first reflections to be heard after the direct sound from a source. Early reflections tell your ears a great deal about the size of a room.

echo. 1. A discrete reflection arriving after the direct sound. 2. A delayed duplicate of the original sound heard after the direct sound.

egg carton. "Home brew" acoustical device, originally designed to transport and store chicken eggs, that provides little acoustical benefit.

eigentone. See *room mode*.

EQ. See *equalizer*.

equalizer. Audio processor that boosts or cuts the level of a particular frequency or range of frequencies. Used to modify the frequency response or tonal shape of the signal being processed.

5.1. Surround sound reproduction system consisting of five identical speakers with a dedicated LFE speaker.

far field. Speakers or a sound source placed beyond the "near field" range (more than three or four feet or so from the listener).

Fast Fourier Transform. A mathematical method for analyzing a waveform that allows for the transfer between the time and frequency domains. Baron Fourier figured out that audio waveforms could be represented as the sum of many component single-frequency waves (sine waves). A Fourier Transform is both the graph showing the frequency content of a waveform and the mathematical equation that can be used to represent it.

FFT. Abbreviation for Fast Fourier Transform.

filter. Audio processor that removes a particular frequency or range of frequencies from a signal.

first reflection. Sound waves that reach the listener's ears after one bounce from a surface, less than 20 milliseconds after the direct sound from the source.

flat. 1. Having an even frequency response without dips or peaks due to electronic or physical characteristics. 2. A device or room in which all frequencies are outputted at unity gain—that is, at the same output level as they came in. Because a flat device or room doesn't emphasize or deemphasize any frequencies, it provides a true picture of the signal that will translate well to other systems and rooms.

float. To suspend the floor of a studio on hard rubber "pucks" to isolate it from the rest of the structure.

floating floor. Floor that is isolated from the surrounding structure.

flutter echo. A fast echo or rattling effect cased by sound waves bouncing between two parallel hard surfaces and creating many fast, discrete echoes.

Fourier, Baron Jean Baptiste Joseph. French mathematician and physicist who developed a method for analyzing periodic functions, such as audio waveforms.

free field. An area with no reflective surfaces. The only true one is outer space, because even outdoors there is the earth to reflect from.

frequency. Number of times a sound wave vibrates, or moves through a complete cycle, in a second.

frequency response. 1. How a device or space responds to a range of frequencies. 2. Maximum and minimum frequencies a device can pass with full level.

frequency sweep. See *sweep.*

fundamental. The "base," "core," or primary frequency of a pitched sound. The fundamental is almost always the lowest frequency component of a given sound.

gain. Amplification applied to a signal, expressed in decibels.

Golden Mean. Ratio of 0.618, which, when applied to room dimensions, is believed by some to provide the ideal spacing of room modes across the frequency response of the space. In practice, this works out to the width being 1.6 times the height, and the length being 2.6 times the height.

Golden Ratio. See *Golden Mean.*

graphic EQ. Type of audio equalizer with a separate level control (usually a slider) for each of a dedicated number of frequencies. Referred to as "graphic" EQ because the curve or arrangement of the control sliders is visually analogous to the response of the unit.

grille cloth. Fabric used to protect and conceal drivers in a speaker cabinet.

harmonic. A tone occurring at an integer multiple of the fundamental's frequency.

harmonic series. One of a series of tones including and related to the fundamental of a tone. The harmonic series consists of integer multiples (1x, 2x, 3x, 4x, etc.) of the fundamental. For example, the harmonics for a 1,000 Hz tone are 1,000 Hz, 2,000 Hz, 3,000 Hz, 4,000 Hz, etc.

Helmholtz, Hermann. German physicist and physiologist who wrote the book *On the Sensation of Tone*.

Helmholtz absorber. An acoustic device consisting of a resonator that vibrates in response to sound waves at a particular frequency or range of frequencies. In practice, a Helmholtz absorber is a box enclosing a volume of air, with a series of slits or holes in one surface. Air motion due to sound waves causes the absorber to resonate in much the same way as blowing across the opening of a soda bottle creates a tone.

Helmholtz device. See *Helmholtz absorber*.

Helmholtz resonator. See *Helmholtz absorber*.

Hertz (Hz). Number of vibrations or complete cycles of a sound wave occurring within a second. Named for Heinrich Hertz.

Hertz, Heinrich. A late-19th-century physicist who first investigated and artificially produced radio waves.

hot spot. Position in a room where there is a boost at a particular frequency or range of frequencies.

HVAC. In construction, heating, ventilation, and air conditioning.

imaging. The ability to localize or pinpoint the position of a sound in a stereo or surround mix when listening.

impulse. A "spike" of sound of a very short duration used to perform acoustical measurements.

impulse response. Literally, how a device or space responds to an impulse. By capturing the response of a room to an impulse, FFT (Fast Fourier Transform) analysis can be performed to obtain frequency-related response information.

infrasonic. Frequencies below the range of human hearing.

inverse square law. Physical law that says that intensity is inversely proportional to the square of distance. In acoustic terms, this results in a 6 dB drop every time you double the distance; 10 times the distance reduces loudness by 20 dB.

isolation. Keeping sound from entering or escaping from a space.

isolation booth. Small room designed to contain, or isolate, the sound of a source so that it can be recorded without bleed to or from other sound sources.

kHz. Abbreviation for kilohertz.

kilohertz. 1,000 Hertz or cycles per second.

LFE. Abbreviation for low frequency effects. The ".1" of a surround sound system, used to carry low-frequency information. The concept is to provide a separate driver and amplifier for the power-intensive low-frequency components of film and video sound effects, such as explosions.

listening position. Where the listener is ideally located when monitoring audio.

live. Reflective, without absorption.

Live-End/Dead-End (LEDE™). Trademarked term for a type of studio design featuring absorption in the front of the room, and reflective surfaces in the rear of the room.

localization. The ability to discern where in a space a sound source is coming from.

loudness. Objectively, the measured SPL (sound pressure level) of a sound. Subjectively, loudness depends on the frequency and timbre of the sound and varies from listener to listener.

machine room. Dedicated room in a studio designed to isolate devices (such as computers, hard drives, and tape machines) that might contribute to an increased ambient noise floor.

MDF. Abbreviation for medium-density fiberboard, a wood product made from processed wood fibers combined with resin and used wherever real wood might be used.

membrane trap. Type of bass trap that features a thin "membrane," panel, diaphragm, or surface that vibrates in response to low-frequency sound waves.

microphone (mic). Transducer that converts sound waves into electrical signals.

midrange. Literally, the middle part of a frequency range. There is no exact range of frequencies defined within the range of human hearing as the "midrange"; it falls somewhere between the low frequencies and the high frequencies.

millisecond (ms). 1/1,000 of a second.

mixer. At its most basic, a device for combining audio signals. Mixers frequently contain sophisticated audio routing and processing capabilities.

modal. Pertaining to room modes.

modal distribution. How modes are spaced across the frequency response.

mode. See *room mode.*

modes of vibration. See *room mode.*

monitor. 1. To listen to audio via speakers. 2. Studio speakers, usually optimized for "flat" frequency response. 3. A computer display.

monophonic. One audio channel.

music. Organized sound.

near field™. Positioning a sound source close to the listener, often defined as less than one wavelength, but usually accepted to be within three to four feet. Though commonly used, "near field" is a trademarked term.

near field monitor. Studio speaker designed to be used in close proximity to the listener. Near field monitors take advantage of the inverse square law, which says that sound level decreases by the square of the distance. The idea is that the monitors are close to the listener, who will hear primarily direct sound, with any reflections being much lower in level (and therefore much less destructive).

node. A position along a wavelength at which there is no motion. Nodes are spaced 1/2-wavelength apart.

noise. Undesired sound that isn't related to any desired sound. (If it is related, it is "distortion.")

noise floor. Level of ambient noise in a room or self-generated noise in a device. Reducing the noise floor increases the dynamic range.

NRC. Abbreviation for noise reduction coefficient. An overall performance rating for an acoustical material derived by averaging the absorption coefficients across a range of octave bands. Because it is derived from an average, it does not include detailed absorption data for the material, and is therefore less useful than the absorption coefficients for most comparisons.

null. A position in a room where a dip in the level of a particular frequency or range of frequencies occurs due to phase cancellation or reinforcement.

oblique mode. Mode created by sound reflecting across all six surfaces (four walls, floor, and ceiling) in a room. Oblique modes are roughly half as strong as tangential modes, and one-fourth as strong as axial modes.

octave. 1. A doubling or halving of frequency. 2. Musical interval of eight diatonic steps.

omnidirectional. In all directions at once. Omnidirectional microphones pick up sound in a spherical pattern, equally well from all directions. Low-frequency speakers tend to be omnidirectional in their dispersion pattern.

out of phase. Relationship in time of two sound waves of the same frequency, where the peaks and troughs in the waveforms don't line up with one another perfectly. If two identical signals are 180 degrees out of phase, the highest peak in one signal exactly lines up with the lowest trough in the other signal, and the two will cancel each other out completely resulting in silence.

overtone. Tones within the sound produced by a source that are higher than, and accompany, the fundamental tone. Overtones may or may not be part of the harmonic series of the fundamental, depending on their mathematical relationship to the fundamental. (Overtones must be integer multiples of the fundamental to qualify as harmonics.)

panel trap. See *membrane trap.*

parametric equalizer. Type of audio equalizer invented by producer/engineer George Massenburg that features separate controls for gain, bandwidth, and frequency for each EQ band.

partial. See *overtone.*

passive monitor. Type of studio speaker that requires an external amplifier.

peak. 1. Literally, the highest point. 2. An area where reinforcement of sound waves causes a boost in level at a particular frequency.

phase. Position in the 360-degree periodic cycle of a waveform.

phase cancellation. Destructive interaction of two identical out of phase sound waves. Phase cancellation results in a reduction or increase in level at a particular frequency due to the two sound waves reinforcing or interfering with one another. If waves are out of phase, the phase of their cycles doesn't line up exactly, and cancellation may occur if they are mixed, resulting in what is often described as a "hollow" sound. How much cancellation occurs depends on how far out of phase the two waves are; 180 degrees is completely reverse phase and results in 100% cancellation. Conversely, 0 degrees and 360 degrees are completely in phase, resulting in the waves summing and reinforcing one another.

phase distortion. Changing the phase relationship of frequencies within a waveform.

pink noise. A type of random noise signal used for testing purposes containing equal energy for each octave. Sounds "bassy" and muffled to our ears. Because of how the energy is distributed in pink noise, it is useful for measuring the frequency response of audio devices as well as rooms and other spaces.

pitch. Musical quality defined by the frequency of a sound wave.

powered monitor. See *active monitor.*

preamp. Electronic device used to raise the level of a signal before the main stage of amplification occurs.

Pro Tools. Computer-based DAW hardware and software system manufactured by Digidesign.

psychoacoustics. The study of how we perceive sound and extract information from acoustics.

quadratic residue diffusor. Acoustical device designed with a random surface pattern using mathematical formulas.

range of human hearing. Generally accepted as 20 Hz to 20,000 Hz.

rarefaction. Area of decreased pressure caused by a sound wave. The opposite of a compression.

rattle. See *flutter echo.*

reflect. To bounce off a surface.

Reflection-Free Zone (RFZ™). Absorbent area in a studio around the main listening position.

reflector. Acoustical device used to redirect sound waves.

resonance. Literally, a tendency to vibrate at a particular frequency. In acoustics, a boost in a particular frequency due to a room mode or standing wave.

resonant frequency. Frequency at which resonance occurs. Every object and every material has a resonant frequency.

resonant mode. See *room mode.*

resonator. Acoustical device that vibrates sympathetically in response to a sound wave.

reverb. See *reverberation.*

reverb time. How long reverb lasts in a room. See also *RT60.*

reverberant decay. Time it takes for the reverb in a room to stop ringing. See also *RT60.*

reverberation. The sound left ringing in a room after the direct sound from the source is silenced. Sometimes mistakenly called "echo," reverberation differs in that it is a wash of reflections that typically does not contain discrete discernible echoes.

room mode. 1. A low-frequency standing wave in a room. 2. An acoustic resonance at a particular frequency in a room. Room modes occur when sound reflects between parallel surfaces and cause anomalies in the room's response.

room within a room. Type of studio construction in which a floating floor is constructed, then walls and ceiling are built on top of that floor, resulting in a room that is isolated from the surrounding structure.

RT60. Abbreviation for Reverb Time-60 dB. The time it takes for the reverberation in a room to drop in level by 60 decibels.

signal path. 1. The route a signal takes through a series of pieces of equipment. 2. The devices an audio signal passes through while being recorded, mixed, or processed in a studio.

sine wave. A type of waveform containing a single frequency—the fundamental—with no harmonics or overtones. A flute produces a tone very close to a sine wave.

slap echo. See slapback.

slapback. 1. An echo resulting from a sound wave reflecting between parallel surfaces. You can test for slap echo by clapping your hands and listening for a discrete echo. 2. A popular echo effect on 1950s-era recordings, also popular on rockabilly and other styles of music.

slatted absorber. see *Helmholtz absorber.*

sound. Vibrations in the range of human hearing.

sound barrier. Material designed to stop the transmission of sound waves.

sound isolation. A more technically correct way of saying "soundproof."

sound pressure level. The volume or loudness of a sound, expressed in decibels. 0 dB as a reference represents the baseline threshold of human hearing. 80 to 90 dB is the range most recording engineers recommend working at in the studio because our ears have the best response at this volume level.

sound transmission class (STC). A rating that can be used to compare the acoustical isolation provided by different materials. In a series of tests, the sound transmission loss for a series of frequencies is plotted on a graph, the resulting curve is compared to a reference curve, and the STC rating is determined. For example, 1/2-inch gypsum board might have an STC rating of 28. It's important to note that STCs of combined materials don't add—so two layers of gypsum board on a wall do not result in an STC of 56. In this particular case, doubling the gypsum board doubles the mass, which results in an STC increase of 6, from an STC of 28 for a single board to an STC of 34 for a double layer of board. Normal conversation can be heard and understood through a material with an STC rating of 25 to 34. An STC of 65 or higher is considered "soundproof" by many listeners.

sound transmission loss (STL). A frequency-dependent rating of the amount of isolation from sound transmission a particular material provides. For example, 1/2-inch gypsum board might have a sound transmission loss rating of 15 decibels at 125 Hertz, meaning that a 125 Hertz sound wave passing through the gypsum board will be reduced in level by 15 decibels.

sound wave. 1. Wave motion created in air (or other material) as a result of vibration of a material in the human hearing range. 2. A cyclical pressure front consisting of a zone of high pressure (compression) followed by a zone of low pressure (rarefaction), followed by high pressure, etc., propagating through air or other material.

soundproof. Impervious to sound waves. Nearly impossible to achieve without extensive construction and expense.

spare bedroom. Common location for a home studio.

speaker. Transducer that converts electrical signals into sound waves.

speed of sound. Through air, 1,130 feet per second, or 343 meters per second.

SPL. See *sound pressure level.*

SPL meter. Device that measures sound pressure level.

standing waves. Sound waves reflecting between two parallel surfaces in a room. Standing waves always negatively impact the response of the room and are controlled using acoustic treatments.

stereo. Two channels of related audio material.

stereophonic. See *stereo*.

subsonic. Technically, traveling at speeds slower than the speed of sound. Often incorrectly used in reference to frequencies below the range of human hearing. See *infrasonic*.

subwoofer. Speaker dedicated to producing low-frequency sound waves, usually below 120 Hz.

supersonic. Technically, traveling at speeds faster than the speed of sound. Sometimes incorrectly used to refer to frequencies above the range of human hearing. See *ultrasonic*.

surround sound. Sound reproduction system with more than two channels of related audio material.

sweep. Continuous playback of a tone smoothly increasing or decreasing in frequency. Also known as a "frequency sweep."

sweet spot. The location in a listening room with the best response and imaging. For stereo, normally the third point in an equilateral triangle with the two monitors.

sympathetic vibration. Vibrations of a particular frequency produced in a material as a result of contact with sound waves of that same frequency. An increase in the volume of the sound caused by the sympathetic vibration is called "resonance."

tangential mode. Room mode caused by sound waves reflecting across four surfaces in a room, such as the four walls or two walls, the ceiling, and the floor. Tangential modes are about half as strong as axial modes and twice as strong as oblique modes.

test tone. A tone of a certain frequency and timbre played back in a room or through a device to help analyze performance or measure response.

timbral. Related to the tonal quality of a sound.

timbre. The tonal quality of a sound.

tone. 1. A distinct musical pitch. 2. The timbral character of a sound. 3. In musical terms, a whole step.

tone sweep. See *sweep*.

transducer. Device that converts one type of energy into another.

transient. A quick, non-repeating waveform that spikes to a higher level than the surrounding sounds or the average level of the signal. Examples include the "pluck" portion of a guitar note, the hammer strike portion of a piano note, and the attack portion of most percussion instruments.

translate. How consistently an audio mix holds up when heard on different playback systems.

transmission loss. See *sound transmission loss.*

trap. See *bass trap.*

tuned absorber. Acoustic device designed and optimized for absorbing sound waves at a particular frequency or range of frequencies.

tweeter. High-frequency transducer in a multi-driver speaker system.

ultrasonic. Frequencies above the range of human hearing.

volume. The loudness of a signal, subject to the perception of the listener.

waveform. 1. Technically, a graph of the voltages of a periodic signal plotted versus time. 2. The "shape" of a sound wave; the waveform defines the timbre of a sound.

wavelength. 1. Technically, the distance between one peak of a sine wave and the next peak. 2. The result of dividing the speed of sound by the frequency of a sine wave. 3. The physical length of a sound wave. Wavelength is important in calculating the modes of a room.

weighting. When measuring, modifying results to (hopefully) match up better with how our ears hear. For example, a curve applied to sound pressure level measurements to more accurately reflect how our ears perceive loudness. Another weighting might compensate for the frequency response of our ear.

wet. A signal with processing, usually artificial reverb.

white noise. A type of random noise signal used for testing purposes containing equal energy for all frequencies. Because the number of frequencies doubles with each higher octave, white noise sounds bright and "hissy" to our ears; there is a build-up of sonic energy in the higher octaves.

woofer. Low-frequency transducer in a multi-driver speaker system.

Index

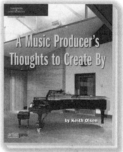

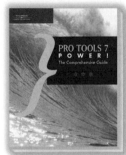